# THE BEAR ESSENTIALS

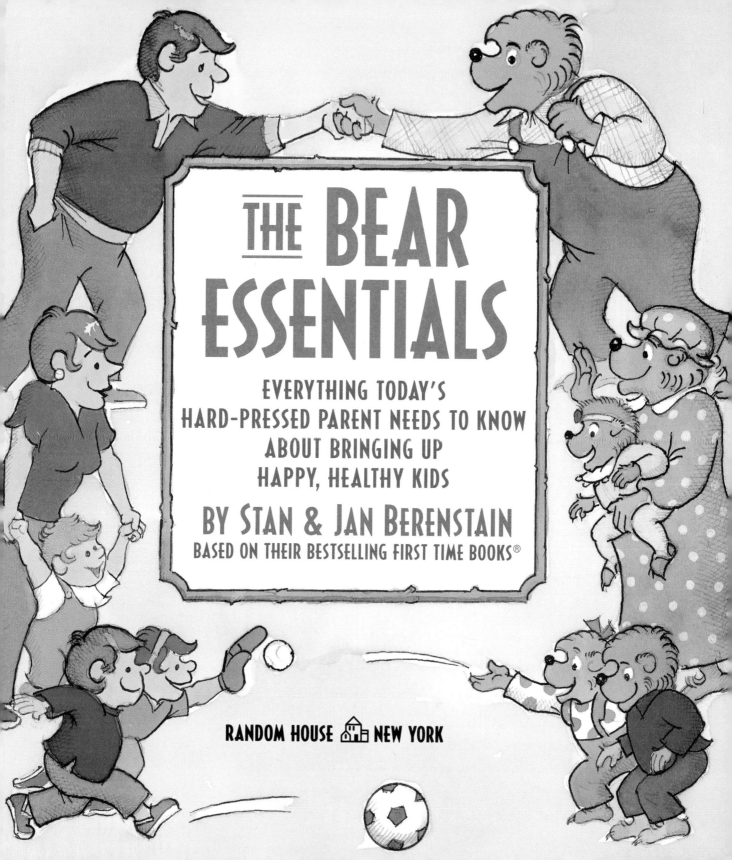

# THE BEAR ESSENTIALS

### EVERYTHING TODAY'S
### HARD-PRESSED PARENT NEEDS TO KNOW
### ABOUT BRINGING UP
### HAPPY, HEALTHY KIDS

## BY Stan & Jan Berenstain
### BASED ON THEIR BESTSELLING FIRST TIME BOOKS®

RANDOM HOUSE 🏠 NEW YORK

www.randomhouse.com/kids
www.berenstainbears.com

*Library of Congress Cataloging-in-Publication Data*
Berenstain, Stan. The bear essentials : everything today's hard-pressed parent needs to know about
bringing up happy, healthy kids / by Stan and Jan Berenstain. — 1st ed.
    p.  cm.
ISBN 0-375-83266-1 (trade pbk.) — ISBN 0-375-93266-6 (lib. bdg.)
1. Child rearing.  2. Child psychology.  3. Parenting.  I. Berenstain, Jan, 1923–  II. Title.
HQ769.B5163  2005  649'.1—dc22  2004008546

Printed in the United States of America  10 9 8 7 6 5 4 3 2 1  First Edition

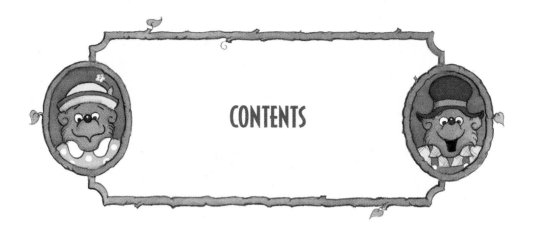

# CONTENTS

# WE GET MAIL!

Through both e-mail and the postal system, we get thousands upon thousands of letters. About half are from kids identifying their favorite character, envying the Bears their tree-house home, or telling us how many dogs, cats, hamsters, and goldfish they have; the other half are from hard-pressed parents seeking further advice on issues we have addressed in our First Time Books® series.

In the Gilbert and Sullivan operetta *Patience,* Colonel Calverley—the very embodiment of military swagger—expounds on the subject of unexpected consequences in his big solo, "When I First Put This Uniform On."

The last thing we expected when we created our funny, furry family ("they're kind of furry around the torso / they're a lot like people, only more so") was to find ourselves pressed into service as experts on the art of parenting. We freely acknowledge that we are without any qualifying licenses or certificates. The only licenses we have are driver's licenses and a marriage license. The only certificates we have are birth certificates and a citation Jan got for perfect Sunday-school attendance.

Nonetheless, on the principle that if the uniform fits, wear it—and given that parents need all the help they can get (from whatever source)—we have tried to do two things in *The Bear Essentials: Everything Today's Hard-Pressed Parent Needs to Know About Bringing Up Happy, Healthy Kids:* (1) give further consideration to the many vexing parenting issues we have addressed in our First Time Books® and (2) provide a First Time Books® guide for parents seeking emergency help from our eponymous Bears.

*Stan & Jan Berenstain*

# NO TWO ALIKE

*"Pumpkins are just like everything else in nature," said Papa Bear as he and the cubs finished weeding the pumpkin patch. "No two of them are exactly alike."*

*"That's for sure," agreed Brother Bear. "Look at that funny flat one and that lumpy one over there." Then there was <u>The Giant</u>, which is what Papa had named one that just seemed to be getting bigger and bigger.*

*"Why is it that no two things are exactly alike?" asked Sister Bear.*

*"It's just the way nature is," answered Papa.*

FROM The Berenstain Bears and the Prize Pumpkin (1990)

Just as each pumpkin in every patch, each leaf on every tree, and each pea in every pod is different one from the other, each and every child that comes pinch-faced and squalling into this world is unique. (Yes, even identical twins. Just ask any mom of identical twins.) Understanding that even the youngest child is an individual with his or her own predispositions, tendencies, and propensities will not only make you a better parent, it is the subtext of virtually every interaction you will ever have with your child.

Parents generally recognize that those anxiety-making charts that appear in magazines that show what your child should be doing at any given age are about as accurate as the age/height/weight charts that appear in those same magazines.

There are children who walk before they talk, children who talk before they walk, and children who run before they do either. There are children who are as tightly wound as a screen-door spring—and others who are as relaxed and languid as a Slinky toy.

There are children that are so soft-spoken that their grandparents never hear a word they say—and those who are so raucous that you can hear them halfway up the next block. There are children who are so shy that they crawl up their mother's leg if you so much as say hello—and others who are so bold that they are in your lap asking how come you have those big hairs in your nose before you can say, "What's your name, little boy?"

Within the bounds of health, safety, and reason, you should permit your children to be themselves. If little Billy insists on keeping his stinky, smelly blankie with him every waking hour, tell yourself that he'll likely put it aside before he enters college.

If little Emily is obsessed with Barbie, consider the possibility that her

Barbie collection may in time become such valuable collectors' items that they may help put her through college.

It's just as important and necessary for you to respect your children for who they are as it is for you to respect your adult family and friends for who they are.

And you may as well, because your children are going to be themselves and eventually go their own way, just as you did when you flew the family coop.

Some further thoughts:

Be wary of one-size-fits-all solutions for problems involving no-two-alike children.

While it's all very well for God to have created humans in His own image, your job as a parent is to give your child the opportunity to be all that he or she can be by being him- or herself.

Provide your child with access to a wide variety of experiences. We are nourished and defined by what interests and excites us. Mark Twain's childhood on the banks of the Mississippi not only put him on the path to literary greatness, it gave him his world-renowned nom de plume. Einstein's immersion in his uncle's clock business led to his interest in the measurement of time and the development of the theory of relativity.

To a great extent, self-esteem comes from a sense of accomplishment. It is therefore a good idea to look with favor on whatever your youngster decides is his or her thing—whether it be bouncing a ball, doing jigsaw puzzles, or learning the names of dinosaurs.

Your child is under no obligation to like the same things you liked in your youth. If your child rejects Raggedy Ann in favor of Yosemite Sam, so be it.

Honoring your child's individuality has nothing to do with permissiveness. The rules are the rules, and they must be respected.

# AND BABY MAKES FOUR

*Down a sunny dirt road, over a log bridge, up a grassy hill, deep in Bear Country, lived a family of bears—Papa Bear, Mama Bear, and Small Bear.*

*It was fun growing up in Bear Country. There were all sorts of interesting things for a small bear to do and see. Small Bear felt good growing up in a tree . . . in his own room . . . in the snug little bed that Papa Bear had made for him when he was a baby. But one morning, it didn't feel so good. Small Bear woke up with pains in his knees and aches in his legs. "Small Bear, you have outgrown your little bed," said Papa Bear. "Today we shall go out into the woods and make you a bigger one!"*

*"But, Papa," called Small Bear, following after him. "What will happen to my little bed?"*

*"Don't worry about that, Small Bear," said Mama Bear as she closed the door after him. She smiled and patted her front, which had lately grown very big and round. "You've outgrown that snug little bed just in time!"*

FROM *The Berenstain Bears' New Baby (1974)*

What excitement! What joy! Hugs, kisses, and congratulations all around! A baby shower! What's more, think pink, because happy, happy day, it's going to be a girl! But just a darned minute. Let's look at the situation from the standpoint of little Billy, the former apple of your eye:

You are a three-and-a-half-year-old and you've got things pretty much under control. It's just you, Mommy, and Daddy, and though they still act out occasionally, you've got them pretty well trained. You've worked your way up through Huggies, Snuggies, and Pull-Ups, and though you still have an accident once in a while, you've hit the big time—the toilet. You've also graduated from crib to bed and from high chair to the dinner table. You let Mommy and Daddy take you places: the zoo, the children's museum, the playground. It's wearing, but they enjoy it, so it wouldn't be fair to deprive them of their pleasure.

But just when you're about to congratulate yourself on managing things so well, a threat no bigger than a basketball appears. It's Mommy's tummy. They say there's a baby inside. There's something in there. You can feel it kick. You guess it's a baby. A wonderful new baby brother or sister, they say. A new baby brother or sister is something you need like a hole in the head.

It's not enough that they've gone ahead and done this without so much as a by-your-leave. Now they're talking about giving the baby your room and moving you into the guest room. Your wonderful room with its cow-jumping-over-the-moon wallpaper, Little Miss Muffet night-light, and counting-sheep mobile. Well, you'll just see about that! Maybe you'll start having accidents in your new grown-up underpants, and maybe you'll start knocking over your milk at the table, and maybe you'll have a terrible time falling asleep at night and need lots and lots of drinks of water.

A wonderful new baby brother or sister, huh?

For starters, it's usually a good idea to let your firstborn decide just how much he wants to know about the new baby and how closely he wants to be involved with your pregnancy.

It may be that little Billy would rather not put his hand on Mommy's tummy and feel the baby kick. If he prefers to keep his distance from Mommy's impersonation of the Goodyear blimp, so be it. Content yourself with letting Daddy feel the baby kick.

Little Emily, on the other hand, who plays Mommy with her dolls every day and feels a certain gender solidarity with Mommy's condition, may be fascinated with the baby's field-goal attempts.

But, in any case, it's best to let your firstborn clue you in on how he or she feels about the arrival of a second child. Children vary considerably in their ability and willingness to accept the situation with equanimity. Some children, usually little girls, just eat the situation up. They're delighted to accompany Mommy on her trips to the doctor. They groove on seeing the baby's fuzzy, indeterminate image on the ultrasound screen. They positively kvell when the doctor fits them with a junior stethoscope and lets them hear the baby's heartbeat. "I hear it! I hear it! It's going ker-*thump*! Ker-*thump*!"

Other children, mostly boys, find the whole baby thing uncomfortable and unnerving. If little Billy would rather lie back in the weeds and look at the situation through the wrong end of a telescope, so be it.

If you press too hard, he might feel it necessary to make his feelings known by peeing on the lovely pink curtains the UPS man just delivered for the baby's room.

Here are some suggestions that may help ease the way as baby makes four.

**Provide your firstborn with plenty of TLC**
But don't overdo it. Avoid emulating the husband who gets into trouble by bringing his wife a dozen roses for no particular reason or occasion and arouses undue suspicion.

**Be calm, cool, and collected—at least, try**

Treat the prospect of an additional member of the family as a simple fact of life. Mommy cats have kittens, mommy dogs have puppies, and mommy humans have babies.

**It depends on the child**

Your firstborn may accept the glad news with angelic equanimity—or he may sprout horns and a tail. It depends on the child. Some kids are so into T-ball, dinosaurs, or Barbie dolls that they couldn't care less about what's happening in Mommy's tummy. Other kids are fascinated by the whole idea of babies and have questions—*lots* of questions.

**Look out for the third rail**

Questions should be answered as simply and as matter-of-factly as you can in the stress of the moment. "Mommies have a special place in their bodies for babies," etc. It may be best at this early stage to avoid the third rail of sex instruction—the part that Daddy plays in the process. There'll be plenty of time for that later. Be prepared, though, with an appropriate answer for the very young child who presses to know, "But how does the baby *get* there?"

**Beware of Uncle Max**

Your firstborn should be protected from inconsiderate relatives. Uncle Max can undo all your good work with a simple remark like, "Hey, Buster. It looks like you're not going to be the big cheese around here anymore."

**Mom's incredible shrinking lap**

Some kids are hypersensitive to environmental change and notice early on that Mommy's lap is getting smaller. This may be the time to gently ask, "Now, why do you suppose that is, sweetie?" There are some kids, on the other hand, who simply don't notice things—not even the fact that Mommy's waist has grown seven sizes. The mother of one such child decided to help things along by using our book *The Berenstain Bears' New Baby* as a conversation starter. The story goes like this: When Small Bear outgrows his baby bed, he and Papa Bear go off into the woods to make a new bed. This happens against the background of pregnant Mama Bear's tummy getting bigger and bigger. Junior was enjoying the story, but he wasn't connecting it with his own mama's shrinking lap. "Sweetie," she said, gently prodding. "What do you suppose Mama Bear has in her tummy?"

"A new bed?" said Junior.

And so, as you feel those first premonitory contractions and drop little Billy off at Gran's and head for the hospital, we move on to your next parenting challenge: persuading your firstborn that being an only child wasn't all that great, and that being a big brother or sister is just about the coolest thing there is.

19

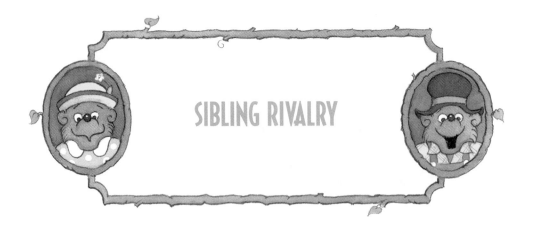

# SIBLING RIVALRY

The Bear family, who lives in the big tree house down a sunny dirt road, has a new member: a baby girl named Honey. What fun! What excitement!

What a nuisance!

Sometimes it seemed that it was crying, feeding, burping, spitting up, and diapering around the clock.

And when it wasn't those things, it was cuddling, dandling, fussing, and kitchy-cooing.

And when it wasn't <u>those</u> things, it was shopping, shopping, and more shopping for things that were needed for the new baby.

It didn't help that when Papa came home from work every day, the first thing he did was pick up the new baby, make goo-goo eyes, and say, "How's my darlin' little dumpling?"

Dumpling. Good name for her, thought Sister—a fat little doughball that was hard to swallow.

It didn't help at all when Aunt Min and Uncle Louie visited and made a big fuss over the new baby.

*It wasn't just Aunt Min and Uncle Louie. It was as if every bear for miles around came to admire the new baby and say how cute she was!*

*"So cute!" said Mrs. Grizzle.*

*"Cute as a bug!" said Mrs. Bruin.*

*"Yeah," snapped Sister under her breath, "a <u>stink</u> bug!"*

*Sister had a point about the new baby being a stink bug. While she couldn't do much, she sure was good at wetting and filling diapers.*

FROM *The Berenstain Bears and Baby Makes Five* (2000)

There is much you can do to help your firstborn accept the new baby, if not with equanimity, at least without open hostility. Here are some thoughts, ideas, and suggestions on how to achieve a non-fratricidal sibling rivalry.

## Be positive

Reject out of hand the negative notion that Junior is bound to be pathologically jealous of the new baby. If you accept the self-fulfilling prophecy that your children's sibling experience is destined to be a rerun of *The Brothers Karamazov* or Cain and Abel, you're licked before you start.

## Get out those baby photos

Having taken the decision to have a second child, you are well advised to prepare your firstborn for the shock and awe of a new baby. At the very least, a familiarization course is in order. A simple way to familiarize your first-born with the endless round of feeding, bathing,

diapering, powdering, salving, burping, fondling, and fussing over that lies ahead is to get out those albums of photos you took of his or her baby days.

Not that you can expect a two- or three-year-old to equate the loving attention he or she received with that due the new baby. But even young children understand the concept of taking turns. They do it every day. They take turns when playing Chutes and Ladders. They take turns on the playground swings. They take turns on Lizzy's hobbyhorse.

Having prepared your firstborn for the new-baby experience, you may find him or her easier to deal with when you are especially busy with the new baby.

"I know how you feel, sweetie," you might venture. "But you had your turn being a baby. Now it's Baby's turn—and say, how would you like to powder the baby's bottom?" Kids can't resist such an invitation. Be wary, however, lest your little helper shake up a choking mushroom cloud of baby powder.

**Passing the "Billy Goats Gruff" test**

Suppose you are nursing your three-month-old and three-year-old Junior decides to test the situation by demanding that you read him "The Three Billy Goats Gruff." Just take a deep breath, bite your tongue, and begin reading. The baby will make an excellent bookrest.

## Lay on beaucoup privileges

It's just as important to have a schedule for your firstborn as it is for your newborn. Laying on a schedule of trips to the zoo, the natural history museum, and the movies with Daddy, Gran, or a favorite aunt or uncle can go a long way toward postponing or preventing the "showdown at Sibling Gap."

## The off-site solution

If there is sufficient separation in age between Johnny-on-the-spot and Jill-come-lately, it may work out that day care or a playgroup is an option. But the timing and handling of such a move is very sensitive. If Junior has even a sneaking suspicion that he is being gotten out from underfoot, he is likely to throw a Rumpelstiltskin.

## Double the trouble

The difficulties of sibling management are doubled when Baby gets up on his or her hind legs and becomes a full-fledged walking, talking, pinching, biting player in the sibling relationship. You may find that the jealousy arrow now points in the other direction. Now the younger sibling is the one that's jealous—jealous of everything about big brother and sister: their toys, their friends, their ability to turn cartwheels and slide down the banister.

Now it's your younger child that needs the laying on of special trips and treats, lest he or she flush some of Junior's favorite Hot Wheels down the toilet while he's away at school.

## Bridging the gap

Playtime with Daddy is a precious commodity.

Question: How can poor, tired old Dad satisfy the needs of both five-year-old Junior and two-year-old Billy at the same time?

Answer: By using his ingenuity and designing games and play activities that are simultaneously satisfying to both children.

Role-playing games are good gap-bridgers. In "Cowboy," for example, Daddy plays the role of Sheriff, Junior plays the role of Cattle Rustler, and little Billy plays the cattle. Here's how the game is played: Sheriff Daddy stomps around shouting, "Whar is that low-down, no-good cattle rustler?" while Cattle Rustler Junior hides the cattle behind the sofa.

This game pattern lends itself to easy adaptation. It can be applied to *Star Trek,* with Daddy serving as Captain Kirk, Junior as Mr. Spock, and Billy as the Klingons.

Or even to Little Red Riding Hood, with Daddy as Little Red Riding Hood, Junior as the Big Bad Wolf, and Billy as Grandma.

The possibilities are endless.

The war between the siblings can be long and enervating, but all you've got to do is stay the course until they become teenagers and turn their attention to their real enemies—Mom and Dad!

No, it's not going to be easy. Nothing about raising kids is easy. But there is no life experience that is more meaningful, more thrilling, more validating than raising kids.

So when the going gets tough, take a deep breath, sit back, and look ahead to the time when your gowned and mortarboarded youngster graduates cum laude from some highly selective university, or your future Nobel Prize winner takes first place in the middle school science fair, or your Title IX athlete becomes the first girl to kick the winning field goal in the Super Bowl.

Hey, you can dream, can't you?

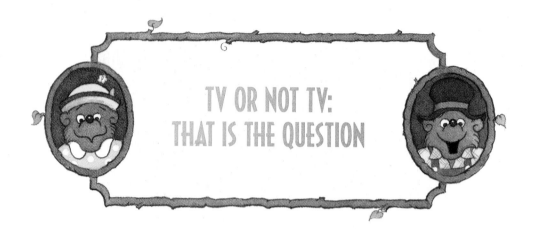

# TV OR NOT TV:
# THAT IS THE QUESTION

Brother and Sister Bear got off the school bus and came into the kitchen with hardly a hello. Then they did what they did every day: They took their milk and cookies into the living room and switched on the TV.

"There's no question about it," thought Mama. "Those cubs are watching too much TV!"

Later, when Papa Bear came in from his shop and joined Brother and Sister, Mama became even more convinced. . . .

"There's absolutely no question about it. The whole Bear family is watching too much TV!"

That evening after dinner, when Brother and Sister scampered in to turn on the TV, Mama stopped them and said her piece: "We've been watching altogether too much television around here!"

"But, Mama," said Brother. "Nutty Bear is coming on and we'll miss it!"

"And The Bear Stooges!" added Sister.

"Well, you'll just have to miss them!" said Mama firmly.

"And furthermore," she added, "you may as well get used to the *idea because there's not going to be any television around here for a whole week!"*

FROM *The Berenstain Bears and Too Much TV* (1984)

The good news about television is that it is the most powerful method of communication ever devised. As it happens, the bad news about television is the same as the good news. It is, indeed, the most powerful method of communication ever devised. Nor is there any doubt that if you should give your child the full use of television that he or she desires, you will find yourself the parent of a small couch potato, fit for nothing more than staring goony-eyed at the business end of a cathode-ray tube.

Of course, there are some television shows that are suitable, even beneficial, for your child—principally the lineup of *commercial-free* children's shows on PBS.

But there are infinitely more children's shows that are, at best, mindless and, at worst, violent, grotesque, inane, and heavily spiced with seductive commercials for food products that induce tooth decay and obesity and for meretricious toys priced to drive Mommy and Daddy to the loan company.

If your youngsters should stumble their way into the tall grass of daytime television, they will be subjected to the ministrations of the

likes of Jerry Springer and Ricki Lake and their panels of sexlorn teenagers whose mothers have stolen their boyfriends.

If, perish forbid, they should wander Hansel and Gretel–like into the nighttime jungle of murder, mayhem, and sex all wrapped around with commercials just this side of X-rated, you may have some very uncomfortable questions to answer.

You'd think it would be safe to watch a major league baseball game with your little T-baller—and it is, until the commercial for a certain gentlemen's product comes on, and we don't mean instant hair color for men.

"What's Viagra, Daddy?" asks little Jack or Jill.

"Er, uh, I believe it's some sort of headache remedy," says Daddy, blushing like a heliotrope.

What's a parent to do?

A few doughty souls have decided for the sake of their children to go without television—to give up the poignant pleasures of Lucy and Desi and *Gilligan's Island,* to forgo the nostalgia of Turner Classics.

But going without television is tantamount to withdrawing from the prevailing culture. For television *is* the prevailing culture. It's one of the only things that are left to hold us together. Exchanges about who got kicked off last night's reality program have all but replaced the weather as the basic topic of social interaction.

Besides, unless you live in the farthest reaches of the Upper Peninsula, it won't do much good to make the sacrifice—forbidden fruit being the most desirable, your child will doubtless feed his or her need by watching television with friends.

But what to do about the big box in the living room?

The best way to protect younger children from the seductions of television is to limit their viewing time to carefully selected programs, then gradually increase their TV time as they grow older.

National surveys tell us that our children watch an average of four to five hours of television a day. That's all very well for the children of Lake Wobegon (where all the children are above average), but if you have higher hopes for your children, you are well advised to join Mama Bear and take a stand against too much TV.

But how much is *too* much?

A very young child needs little or no TV. What your crawler/toddler needs is roll-around-on-the-floor time, commune-with-dust-bunnies time, pull-yourself-up-to-a-standing-position-and-shout-for-joy time, make-a-tower-of-blocks-and-knock-them-down time. In short, he or she needs time to do the things that give a child a sense of accomplishment, which generates that much-desired feeling—hushed pause—*self-esteem!*

Children sometimes ask to interview us for their school newspapers. Question: Why do you just draw bears? Answer: We don't. We draw trees and flowers and birds and so forth. Question: Where do you get your ideas? Answer: From our everyday experiences. Question: How did you think of the name Berenstain Bears? Answer: We didn't. It was our first editor, Theodor Geisel, aka Dr. Seuss, who named the Berenstain Bears. Turnabout being fair play, we often counter-interview them after the usual round of questions and answers.

We began one counter-interview by asking the group of third and fourth graders about their reading preferences. What did they like to read? Dr. Seuss, Judy Blume, Beverly Cleary, they answered. The Berenstain Bears, offered a candidate for the diplomatic corps. How about television? Did they watch television? Sure, they watched television. What shows did they watch? A gallimaufry of TV shows was shouted out. What did they like better—reading books or watching television? A set of blank looks. The question made no sense to them. "Reading books and television are different," suggested one youngster. "How so?" we asked. "Well," ventured another, "when you read a book, it's like you *did* something. When you watch television, it's fun, but, well, it's like you didn't do anything."

*Touché!* we said to ourselves.

That's the point about television. Children need to *do* things—not watch others do things. They need to run and jump and climb. They need to draw pictures and splash paint. They need to learn that they are not the center of the universe by interacting with other children. They need to employ all of their senses to put together some working model of the world.

None of those things is going to happen to a youngster who spends the better part of the day consuming trans-fatty snacks and sucking down sticky, sweet soda while watching the business end of a television tube.

Except for the general dictum that the younger the child, the more parents need to limit viewing time, there is no formula for measuring just how much TV is good or bad for your child. Parents know their children as no one else can. It's up to them to decide how much and which television programs children should be permitted to watch.

Remember that no two children are alike. There are children, believe it or not, who are so energetic and tightly wound that they're not very interested in television. Conversely, there are kids who seem to be natural-born glow-worms who will watch as much TV as you'll let them.

Should expanded TV time be allowed occasionally—for a special program about dinosaurs or a figure-skating show? Of course. Even a very occasional Saturday-morning debauch is not entirely beyond the pale.

But where children and television are concerned, *caution* should be the watchword, lest your youngster fall prey to that ghastly condition known as "television dependency," a condition for which there is no twelve-step program.

Below are some further thoughts and suggestions.

### Watch TV with your kids—yes, even Barney

Even the most innocent and well-intentioned children's programs can raise questions in your child's mind. Questions such as: Why is Clifford the Big Red Dog so big? And why does Oscar the Grouch live in a trash can? And why do they say Barney the Dinosaur is purple when he's really magenta? You should be there to answer such questions.

### Consider your own viewing habits

Your youngster is far more likely to do what you do than what you say. So it might be a good idea to take a considered look at your own TV viewing habits. If you are a TV junkie, there's a better-than-average chance that your youngster will acquire the habit.

**Inoculate your kids against advertising**

Since commercials are unavoidable once you wander off the PBS reservation, it's necessary to explain the nature of advertising to younger viewers. The explanation should be simple—something along the following lines: People who are trying to sell things sometimes stretch the truth a little.

**Too much TV can be hazardous to your children's health**

Television viewing isn't necessarily fattening, but it is tremendously so if accompanied by constant snacking and a sedentary lifestyle. It's a good idea

to keep abreast of research findings about the effects of television on children. For instance, recent research suggests that watching too much TV, especially when children are young, may actually affect the developing brain such that certain learning problems may result. So, parents, stay well-informed—and stay tuned!

### It's a TV jungle out there

We used to put the garbage out on the curb. Now it comes into our homes over cable and through the ether. Channel surfing in today's TV market is definitely not for kids. So retain command of the remote control at all times.

### We love Lucy

As your youngster gets older, you may want to let him or her in on such retro shows as *I Love Lucy, Gilligan's Island, The Munsters,* and *I Dream of Jeannie.* They're funny, they're family-friendly, and they're singularly free of double entendres and other question-begging content.

# OVERCOMING FEARS

Papa took Sister's hand. "Come with me," he said.

"Where are we going?" she wanted to know.

"Up to the attic."

"The attic? But it's dark in the attic—even in the daytime."

"I know," said Papa. "But there's something I want to show you. Anyway, there's nothing so special about the dark. It's just part of nature, like the light. It's your imagination that makes the dark seem spooky sometimes."

"What's imagination?" asked Sister.

"Imagination is what makes us think that chests of drawers and clothes trees are cave creatures."

"I wish I didn't have one," said Sister.

"Don't say that," said Papa. "A lively imagination is one of the best things a cub can have. It's imagination that lets us paint pictures, make up poems, invent inventions! The trick is to take charge of your imagination—and not let it take charge of you."

When they got to the attic, Papa began to rummage through boxes, looking for something.

*"Here it is!" said Papa. "My old night-light! The one I used when I was a cub and had a little trouble falling asleep in the dark!"*

*Sister couldn't quite believe that her big, powerful papa was ever afraid of the dark.*

*"Oh, sure," said Papa. "Most of us are at one time or another."*

FROM *The Berenstain Bears in the Dark* (1982)

With "spooky stuff" having become so pervasive a part of entertainment culture, it's inevitable that you are going to have to put in occasional night duty as your child's personal exorcist. And while you have no obligation to become a full-fledged parapsychologist, it would be good to think a bit about how you will deal with your youngster's concerns about ghosts, goblins, and monsters.

Here are some thoughts and ideas for your consideration.

**Get an early fix on your child's sensitivity to "spooky stuff"**

Kids are just as different in their susceptibility to imaginary fears as they are in other ways. Some infants are spooked by anybody less familiar than Mama, while others gleefully call every man "Dada." Assess your child's ability to deal with stories and TV shows in which threat, danger, and conflict figure. If the likes of the Big Bad Wolf and the troll from "The Three Billy Goats Gruff" spook your very young child, consider backing off for the likes of "The Three Little Kittens" and *Goodnight Moon* for a while—for your own sake as well as your

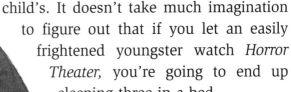

child's. It doesn't take much imagination to figure out that if you let an easily frightened youngster watch *Horror Theater*, you're going to end up sleeping three in a bed.

**If your child is afraid of the dark, try leaving the lights on**

It is astonishing how many parents decide to make the lights-off/lights-on question a "battle" issue. A child will fight you on any ground you choose—and will usually win.

If a child is going through a difficult "night fears" period, leaving the lights on for a few nights won't destroy your parental authority. A three-way bulb or rheostat lamp unceremoniously dimmed each night will usually help work through the problem. A friendly night-light or a light left on in the hall are other obvious expedients. Most kids, if you give them half a chance, will eventually work through imaginary fears.

**The monster in the closet is imaginary, but the fear is real**

Telling a frightened youngster that the monster in his closet is all in his imagination is about as helpful as telling a migraine sufferer that the pain is all in his head. This sort of fear is best dealt with through friendly but matter-of-fact demonstrations of the vacant nature of the closet—plus some kindly distraction: warm milk (no cookies, please; it mustn't get to be *too* much fun) and perhaps an extra teddy bear or two to sleep with.

**Some children are able to work out their fears through creative play**

Does the wicked witch in *Snow White* give your child fits? Get out the Magic Markers and the giant scribble pad and encourage Junior to draw some weird, wild, fantastical witches. React enthusiastically: "That's a wonderful witch, sweetie—I especially like that big wart on her chin. And that long, curly hair growing out of it is pure poetry!" Ditto with modeling clay. And with modeling clay, you have the additional advantage of being able to bash the wicked thing into an amorphous lump after you've had your way with her.

**Some kids really do love monsters and such and thrive on them**

Some youngsters just love the whole idea of ghosts, monsters, spooks, and all kinds of things that go bump in the night. Sometimes it is a child's way of dealing with fears, but as often as not, it is just a harmless, even mindless, preoccupation. Just as some kids are dinosaur-crazy or Barbie-happy, others are monster-mad, and as long as it doesn't give *you* nightmares, it is probably nothing to worry about.

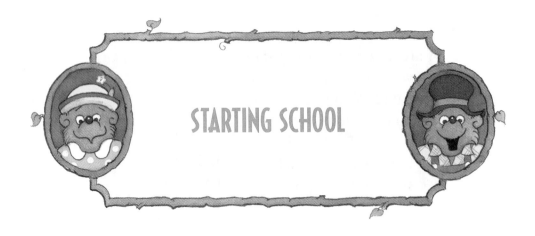

# STARTING SCHOOL

One evening at supper, Brother Bear said, "I'm getting tired of summer vacation. I think I'm ready to go back to school!"

"That _is_ good news," said Papa Bear. "Because school will be starting again, very soon!"

Sister Bear's ears perked up at the word school.

This year Sister would be starting school. And she wasn't quite sure how she felt about it.

She liked being at home with her mother and father . . . her books and toys . . . and her friends.

"What will school be like, Mama?" she asked at bedtime.

"You'll find out tomorrow," said Mama as she tucked Sister in and kissed her good-night.

But when the big morning came, Sister began to worry.

"Mama!" she said. "What if I don't like school? What if I just don't like it?"

FROM _The Berenstain Bears Go to School_ (1978)

Life is a continuum, to be sure. But as we move along its course, there are significant life-changing moments of demarcation: coming of age, marriage, parenthood. None is more life-changing for your child and you than the first time Junior gets on the big yellow bus and goes off to school. Not day care or nursery school or kindergarten, but real all-day school, where bullies roam the schoolyard, where you have to line up according to size, where you have to sit in a certain seat while the teacher talks and talks . . . and talks.

You have been little Billy or Sally's first teacher for six long years. You have gotten your child through the terrible twos, the traumatic threes, and the ferocious fours. You've gotten him or her through childhood diseases, trips to the emergency room, and a family crisis or two. Now you're expected to turn this precious creature, the fruit of your womb, over to a complete stranger.

That's right, a complete stranger! A person of uncertain age, unknown origin, and indeterminate training.

"Oh my God! Here comes the school bus!" cries Mom, coming down with a separation-anxiety attack on the crucial morning. "Oh dear, quick! Kiss Mommy goodbye and hurry down to the school-bus stop where those other children are waiting. But wait! I'll come with you."

By now Mom has pumped Junior into a separation-anxiety attack of his own.

It doesn't have to be that way. Yes, there is bound to be a certain amount of stress when a child goes off to school for the first time. But there are ways to ease the tension, to smooth the transition from Mama's little darling to student with shining morning face going off to school.

Here are some thoughts and ideas that may help.

**Getting your child ready for school**

In one of his short stories, James Thurber tells about going to the movies when he was a child in Columbus, Ohio. There was a man who sat in the balcony, and just when the movie was about to come on, he would shout, "GET READY!"

That's the key to helping your youngster get off to a good school start: *getting ready*.

As regards Mom's concern about entrusting her precious child to a complete stranger, that's her issue to work through. Schools open to prepare for the new school year at least two weeks before school starts. A call to the office explaining that you'd like to bring your soon-to-be first grader to school for a get-acquainted visit and perhaps a hello with his future teacher will almost certainly be welcomed. School folk really appreciate interested parents.

If little Billy or Sally seems relatively relaxed about starting school, an unannounced visit to the school grounds or even a simple drive-by may be sufficient to reduce any anxiety your youngster may harbor.

Getting your child ready for school will be less of a problem if he or she has already been a half-day kindergartner at the school.

However, the experience of kindergarten is as different from that of first grade as singing the alphabet song is different from writing your name on the top line in the upper left-hand corner of your paper.

**Let's not forget about Daddy**

As if things are not touchy enough during the

run-up to Junior's first day of school, who should blunder onto the scene but Daddy. He has somehow sensed that something important is about to happen and, calling on his animal cunning, has figured out that Junior is going into first grade.

"What happened to kindergarten? Don't they go to kindergarten first?" he asks, sniffing the air with his trunk, his great ragged ears rippling in the light breeze.

"He *went* to kindergarten."

"With all the finger painting and blocks and everything?"

"Yep."

"Hmmm."

The great beast is perturbed.

The training of the young is a serious matter. Has he allowed the female to take too much upon herself? Perhaps it's not too late. With a shake of his great head, he lumbers over to where Junior is grazing at the edge of the herd and addresses him. "Son"—advice to young elephants: When they start calling you "Son," look out—"Son, I understand you're about to enter first grade. Everything you do in school from now on goes into your permanent record. You've got a good mind and a good background, so there's no reason why you shouldn't be at the top of your class. Do I make myself clear? NOW, YOU GO RIGHT INTO THAT FIRST GRADE AND *DO A JOB*!" he bellows, and crashes off through the underbrush.

And what does Junior do? He goes right into the first grade and does a job. He throws up all over the place.

**What an entering first grader is expected to know**

Generally speaking, first-grade teachers expect entering students to know left from right (something some of us are never quite sure of), know how to write their names, be able to count, have a working knowledge of the alphabet, and be able to sit still for more than five minutes.

First-grade teachers also know that the members of each incoming first-grade class will exhibit a wide variety of capabilities. At one extreme there'll be little Esme, who has been reading the *Encyclopaedia Britannica* since she was two and can recite the names of Henry the Eighth's six wives in succession, noting which two went to the block. At the other extreme there's big Rudolf, who furrows his brow when you ask his name.

Billy or Sally will probably more than meet the teacher's expectations—it's not for nothing that you let them watch *Sesame Street*.

In first grade your child will learn more about numbers than how to count, more about getting along with others than pushing and shoving, and more about following instructions than you ever thought possible. But the main event in first grade is reading.

The method of teaching reading used in most schools is a time-tested combination of phonics and the word method. Most first-grade teachers divide their reading classes into three groups according to ability. Comparisons being odious, the teacher avoids them by giving the groups value-free names like The Bluebirds, The Cardinals, and The Robins. But the kids aren't fooled.

Neither is Mom. "Which reading group are you in, dear?" she asks.

"I'm in The Cardinals," says Junior. "That's the dumb group."

Lest Mom think that Junior is being consigned to the scrap heap, she should be reminded that the teacher is *not*—repeat, *not*—saying Junior is dumb. What she may be saying is that, for any number of reasons, Junior may not be as ready for reading as some of the other kids. It won't hurt to talk to the teacher about it if you are concerned. It may be that a little low-pressure reading work on the home front would be useful.

Or the teacher might say "not to worry" and point out that Billy or Sally is the youngest child in the class.

It is good to remember, when you are tempted to compare Junior's progress with that of others in the class, that the youngest child in any first grade is going to be up to 18 percent younger than the oldest child—an enormous gap, especially at this rapidly changing stage of development.

**Establish good homework habits early**

First grade doesn't ease into homework. First grader Billy or Sally will begin bringing home assignments almost immediately upon the start of the school year.

Homework will be an important part of you and your child's life from here on, right up through high school. So it's a good idea to establish good homework habits from the first day of school.

How you fit homework into your family schedule is up to you and Junior, just so you establish a regimen that's regular and mandatory. The amount of homework required through the years may vary from teacher to teacher, from course to course. But one thing is certain: the most often cited reason for academic failure is falling behind in homework.

**Your local school needs you**

Lots of moms (and not a few dads) are able to pitch in and help out at school. Something as simple as helping to chaperon Billy's or Sally's school trip to the zoo, art museum, or farm can help.

Perhaps you have some special skill or qualification. It's been a while since you co-captained your high school field hockey team. But you might consider helping coach your daughter's team. Not only will she puff up with pride and say, "That's my mom!" but running around with the girls may take off an unwanted pound or two.

Is Daddy as handy with tools as Norm Abram of *This Old House*? If so, he can help build stands and booths for the big spring fund-raiser.

Perhaps you can man the office phone one afternoon a week, or do yard duty one morning a week, or help organize the annual bake or clothing sales.

With school budgets being cut and school bond initiatives being voted down willy-nilly, schools need all the extra help they can get.

Of course, you're volunteering out of a high-minded sense of civic duty, but having an in won't hurt if you should need some sort of dispensation from the principal, like being permitted to take Billy or Sally out of school a week early for a spring vacation.

**Homeschooling**

According to the American Homeschool Association, about 4 percent of the nation's kids are homeschooled. That may be a small percentage, but it is a heckuva lot of kids.

The advantage of homeschooling is that it avoids having your kids exposed to the competitive, test-driven, religion-free, government-approved, ethnically and racially diverse—and divided—nature of today's public schools.

The *dis*advantage of homeschooling is that it avoids having your kids exposed to the competitive, test-driven, religion-free, government-approved, ethnically and racially diverse—and divided—nature of today's public schools.

Parents choose to homeschool their children for a variety of reasons. A substantial portion does so for religious reasons. Such parents believe so strongly that religion must be an integral part of a child's education that they homeschool. It is a considerable job, one that is complicated by the fact that each state has a different set of educational requirements.

Some parents choose to homeschool because, in their judgment, their child's educational needs are so far in advance of what the local school can provide that they have no choice but to homeschool.

Isolation and physical disability are other reasons that parents choose to homeschool. Parents' right to do so is fully protected under the U.S. Constitution, provided they fulfill the requirements of the specific state.

Notwithstanding that it is a right, there is always the issue of whether the homeschooled child misses out on the socialization and acculturation that come with rubbing up against the multi-ethnic, multi-racial world at large.

Wherever and however you school your child, there is nothing better that you can do than to see that he or she receives the great enabling boon and blessing of education.

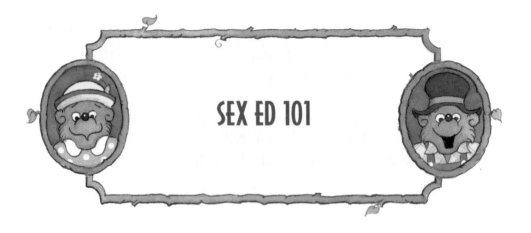

# SEX ED 101

*"I guess you've noticed that birds and bears and bunnies and deer all come in males and females," said Mama.*

*"Yes," said Sister. She remembered from when she and Brother were very little and used to take baths together.*

*"Well," said Mama, "it's not just birds and bears that come in males and females. Some trees and flowers do, too."*

*"You mean there are boy and girl trees and flowers?"*

*"More like male and female," said Mama. "But that's the general idea. And while the honeybees are gathering nectar to make honey, they're doing another important job. They're picking up pollen from the male flowers and carrying it to the female flowers. It's the female flowers that make the seeds that grow into more flowers."*

*Sister could accept that.*

FROM *The Birds, the Bees, and the Berenstain Bears (2000)*

Sooner or later—and it had better be sooner rather than later—you are going to have to teach your children about sex.

It's a dirty job, but somebody's got to do it. If you don't, everybody else will: radio shock jocks, the Super Bowl halftime show, hip-hop lyrics, and just about any prime-time sitcom you'd care to name.

Will you have difficulty telling your little dear about the torrid tango that Havelock Ellis called "the Dance of Life"? Probably. Will the stutter you thought you'd overcome reassert itself? Possibly. Will there be moments of truth when your youngster fixes you with a basilisk eye and nails you with tough questions? Sample tough question: "Look, Mom, I understand that the mommy has an egg and the daddy has a seed and they make a baby in the mommy's tummy. But what I want to know is how the daddy's seed gets into the mommy's tummy in the first place." *Count* on tough questions.

But the tough questions probably won't come up until you've had time to prepare for them.

There is no need to give away the whole show prematurely. The oft-repeated dictum "Answer the child, not the question" is a pretty good place to start. Your answers should be simple, straightforward, and age-appropriate. Evasiveness and artful dodging are to be avoided. They'll just prompt your little sex researcher to seek answers elsewhere—and heaven only knows what Junior might pick up on the school bus.

The error of overanswering is best demonstrated by one of the oldest sex-ed jokes in the book:

Little Billy comes in from playing with Herbie and asks the classic question, "Mommy, where did I come from?" Mommy—who has been reading up on the subject and waiting anxiously for him to pop the question—immediately launches into a hyperdrama about "spunky spermatozoons" fighting their way up fallopian tubes until, in a last desperate spasm of flagellations, one lucky guy thrusts his way into a ripened ovum, etc., etc., *ad infinitum,* until the little twosome fastens itself on to the blood-rich wall of the uterus, where they make beautiful music together until they grow into a baby and emerge triumphant into a waiting world.

MOMMY, WHERE DID I COME FROM?

"It's called the miracle of birth," says Mommy. "Well, does that answer the question of where you came from?"

"Well," says little Billy, looking mildly baffled, "I was playing with Herbie, and when we got to talking about where we came from, he said he came from Pittsburgh, and I just wanted to know where I came from."

Silence.

Mom waits for the rim shot from the drummer. But there is no drummer, so she just stands there with her face hanging out.

But let's rerun the tape and give Mom another chance: Billy, once again, comes in from playing with Herbie and asks, "Mommy, where did I come from?" Mom is a little cagier the second time around, and a little more cautious.

"Er," says Mom. "Tell me something, sweetie. Where did Herbie say *he* came from?"

"Pittsburgh," says Billy.

"Well, then," says Mom. "You can tell Herbie that you come from right here in good old Punxsutawney."

Can you do real damage by telling a child too much, too soon? One mother thought so and sought reassurance from us. We were on the road promoting a book titled *How to Teach Your Children About Sex Without Making a Complete Fool of Yourself.* It was based on our own awkward attempts to teach the Berenstain children about sex. We were on a TV talk show that took questions from the audience. As we sat there on the couch with the host and co-host, the voice of a troubled mom came to us over the loudspeaker.

"I had a situation come up with my nine-year-old daughter, and I'm not sure I handled it very well. I'd like to know what your guests think about it."

"What sort of situation?" asked the host.

"Well," said Troubled Mom, "my daughter came into our room at an inopportune time and sort of, you know, caught us. . . . She was pretty upset, so I, you know, told her the whole story—you know, what Daddy does to Mommy to make a baby and all that. And she said—and this is what worries me—'*Oh, Mommy, I'm never going to do that!*' Do you think I did her any real harm?"

Silence hung in the air of the cavernous studio. The host was open-mouthed, but no words came. Ditto the co-host, who happened to be a former nun who had gone over the wall. The male member of Team Berenstain had lockjaw. But wise Mama Bear had a reassuring answer. "I wouldn't worry about it," she said. "I think she'll change her mind."

And no doubt she will.

One of Mark Twain's many bon mots is on the subject of weather: "Everybody talks about the weather, but nobody does anything about it."

With sex, it's quite the other way. Not everybody talks about sex, but everybody does something about it. Including your kids. So there's little time to lose. Here are some thoughts and ideas that may help you get the job done.

**Coming to terms with terms**

Introduce correct anatomical terms fairly early. Nothing gets old more quickly than cutesy names for body parts. While it's natural enough to hark back to the baby terms of your own childhood when your kids are very young, it's usually a good idea to dispense with them as soon as you are comfortable using the proper terms.

It's difficult enough to talk about sex with kids, especially as they grow older, without having to resort to idiotic diminutives for parts that are no longer diminutive. To the parents who anticipate having a problem saying words like *penis, vagina,* and *scrotum,* we offer the same advice a New Yorker gave an out-of-towner who asked how to get to Carnegie Hall. The advice: *Practice, practice, practice!* In front of a mirror, if necessary. Try not to get caught at it, though.

## KISS (Keep It Simple, Stupid)

Keep in mind that until they are about five years old, kids have no idea that their sexual questions are loaded. They are merely part of the general run of questions kids ask. Do thousand-leggers have a thousand legs? (Not really—one hundred pairs is the correct answer.) Why is the sun red when it comes up in the morning? (It is being viewed through the distorting lens of Earth's atmosphere.) Why does the moon look so big when it's low and so small when it's high? (That's a good one to ask your daddy when he gets home.) Your best course is to answer your child's sex-related questions in a simple, straightforward, age-appropriate manner.

## It's different now

When Hector and we were pups and fear of pregnancy was enough to keep the sexual revolution at bay, most pubescent kids made do with necking and petting. It's different now. For both parents and kids. And while it's not quite the apocalypse, we're getting close. What's a parent to do?

## Educate yourself

One thing you can do is educate yourself. Find out what you need to know to adequately educate your kids on such subjects as human sexuality and reproduction, failure (and success) rates of various kinds of birth-control products, the dangers of date rape, sexually transmitted diseases, and that terrifying disease with the ironically positive-sounding acronym—AIDS.

## Avoid scare tactics

If kids scared easily, they wouldn't be the only population segment in which smoking is on the increase. Present your material about sexually transmitted diseases and unwanted pregnancy in a calm, factual, nonpatronizing manner.

## The abstinence/condom dichotomy

However you approach the subject of unwanted pregnancy with your kids, the birth control–versus–abstinence issue is bound to come up. One way to deal with this difficult dichotomy without completely begging the question is to impress on them what a remarkably effective baby-making machine the human reproductive system is—and that unprotected sex is the reproductive equivalent of playing Russian roulette with all the chambers filled. It's not an accident when you get pregnant; it's an accident when you *don't*.

## You are the one

When it comes to the crucial, compelling, and consequential area of sex, you are the one!

Only you are in the position to follow the biblical injunction "Train up a child in the way he [or she] should go." Only you are in the position to arm your son or daughter against the sexual peer pressure that inevitably coincides with puberty. Only you know your daughter well enough to decide whether you can successfully make the case for abstinence. Only you can inoculate your son against the ugly and destructive macho code of counting sexual coups. And only you are standing at ground zero of the continuous, ubiquitous sexplosion with which your youngster must cope.

But don't panic. Just hang in there and take your best shot.

# EXPLETIVES DELETED— PLEASE!

*Sister Bear was just beginning to wonder what to do with herself one afternoon when the phone rang.*

*It was Lizzy Bruin asking her to come over to play.*

*"Bring your dolls with you," said Lizzy. "We'll play house. And, later on, we can watch a video."*

*Sister put her dolls in their stroller and hurried over to Lizzy's.*

*Lizzy was waiting for her at the door and helped her carry the dolls upstairs to her room. Sister and Lizzy had been playing house with their dolls the last time Sister visited, so they just picked up where they left off.*

*As the game went on, the dolls got into an argument and began shouting (it was really Sister and Lizzy pretending to be the dolls who were doing the shouting). The game got so loud that Lizzy's mom asked them if they could play more quietly. They decided to watch a video that Lizzy's older brother had rented. It was called* Trouble at Big Bear High *and it looked pretty grown-up.*

*It was all about teenagers in high school. They used a lot of words Sister didn't understand. Whenever the teenagers got angry or upset, they used words Sister never heard before. She figured that these words were sort of like "Phooey!" or "Fudge!" but more grown-up.*

*That evening at dinner at the tree house, Sister was telling the family about the video. When she got to the exciting part, she waved her hand and knocked over her milk. It spilled all over the table.*

*She was about to say "Oh, phooey!" or "Oh, fudge!" but one of the words from the video popped into her head and she said it real loud.*

*There was a pause. Mama, Papa, and Brother stared at her with their mouths open.*

*Uh-oh, thought Sister.*

FROM *The Berenstain Bears and the Big Blooper (2000)*

One of the inconveniences that come with parenthood is the necessity of cleaning up your language around children. Indeed, you will find to your

frequent embarrassment that your youngster is a virtual feedback mechanism when it comes to reproducing any bad language he or she may overhear.

Short of resorting to pig Latin or swearing in French (even that is dangerous given children's well-recognized facility with language), the simplest solution to the problem is to expunge all inappropriate language from your vocabulary.

But old habits die hard.

In order to forestall the use of inappropriate language, you may find it necessary to establish a schedule of penalties for language slips. The effectiveness of such a schedule will be enhanced if the offending parent is required to pay the non-offending parent. Such a penalty schedule might look something like this:

### Penalties for the use of profane, vulgar, or otherwise inappropriate language

| | |
|---|---|
| The d-word (*damn*) | 25¢ |
| Invoking the Deity | 50¢ |
| Any vulgar scatological term | 75¢ |
| Gratuitous reference to nether body parts | $1.00 |
| The f-bomb | $2.00 |
| Losing it completely | $5.00 |

Given the male propensity for blasphemous locker-room language, the above may seem unfair to Daddy. But whoever said life was fair?

Cleaning up your own language is all very well. But what about the coarsening, vulgarizing effect of outside influences?

Here are some thoughts and ideas that may help you hold back the flood.

Make it clear to your youngster that you are no more willing to accept the "bad words" he or she brings home than you are the dead birds, live snakes, and stray cats he or she brings home.

Your little one may be using swearwords in all innocence. If so, be prepared to explain what they mean. But more important, be prepared to explain why people use them (feel free to consult Mama Bear's speech on the subject to Sister Bear in *The Big Blooper* for tone and approach).

Hold your ground against accusations that you are old-fashioned or even a goody two-shoes.

Without being hysterical or a bore about it, let your kids know that there's a difference

between funny and vulgar—that you don't consider Bart Simpson's assertions that everything "sucks" all that funny.

You are well within your parental rights to proscribe any TV show you regard as excessively vulgar. A difficulty with such a proscription is that the way things are going, you may be reduced to watching the Weather Channel, Animal Planet, and *Mr. Rogers* reruns.

Though you may occasionally feel like King Canute trying to hold back the sea, all is not lost. There is a rising tide of parental protest against the coarsening of our culture. Parental protests notwithstanding, even formerly respectable institutions have joined the pander parade. In the recent past, network sitcoms at least had the grace to indulge in double entendres. Now they go straight for the groin with *single* entendres.

That venerable institution, the *New York Times,* has routinely included a book about a flatulent dog on its children's bestseller list.

Granted that the *f* word for flatulence does have standing as Middle English, but so do all those other four-letter Middle English words that up to now the *New York Times* has not deemed fit to print.

If the *Times* felt that it was absolutely necessary to bring the news about Walter, they might have, at least, had the grace to employ the initial consonant device—i.e., "Walter, the F_ _ _ _ _ Dog." On second thought, that wouldn't have been such a good idea either.

And speaking of publishing, many of the country's largest children's book publishers have taken to scattering all sorts of bathroom and anatomical humor through their children's lists.

We recognize that children have been engaging in bathroom humor since long before there were bathrooms, and they will continue doing so. To quote a Seinfeldian phrase on another subject, "Not that there's anything wrong with it." Bathroom humor is part of a natural and normal developmental stage for children. But they are perfectly capable of engaging in it without any encouragement from adults.

Would we like to turn back the clock to an earlier time? The answer is yes.

Which earlier time?

How about yesterday?

And if this be goody two-shoes fuddy-duddyism—so be it!

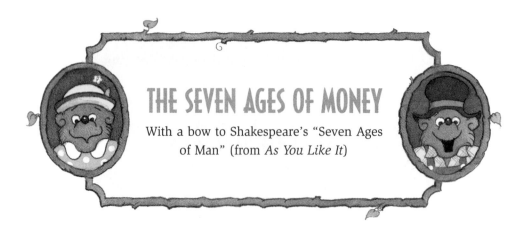

# THE SEVEN AGES OF MONEY

With a bow to Shakespeare's "Seven Ages of Man" (from *As You Like It*)

*Money wasn't a big problem in the Bear family's tree house down a sunny dirt road deep in Bear Country. But it <u>was</u> a problem—at least where cubs Brother and Sister were concerned. They knew some things about money. They knew that Papa wasn't made of it, that it didn't grow on trees, and that they should save it for a rainy day. Papa had told them those things many times. What they didn't know about money was how to manage it.*

*The cubs liked money. They had liked it even before they knew you could buy things with it. They liked coins better than paper money because you could do things with coins.*

*They liked to roll them. They liked to spin them. They liked to stack them.*

*As they got a little older, they liked to play "heads or tails" with them.*

*But by keeping their eyes and ears open at the supermarket, the hardware store, and the clothing store, they soon learned that you could do a lot more with money than just play with it. You could buy things with it.*

*You could buy all sorts of things. Ice cream from the Good Humor Bear, rides on the Bucking Duck at the mall, balloons from the balloon bear at the park.*

*And while they were still fond of coins, they learned that you could buy a lot more with dollars.*

*But when Brother explained that he needed money for baseball cards and Sister explained that she needed money for a wedding dress for her Bearbie Doll, Papa got upset.*

*"Baseball cards? Wedding dress?" shouted Papa. "You must think I'm made of money. You must think money grows on trees!" The cubs backed away. All they wanted was some green money. All they got was Papa red in the face.*

*Mama had been watching. She knew it was time to calm things down, and she had an idea how to do it.*

*"If you cubs will excuse us," she said, "there are some things I'd like to discuss with your papa."*

FROM *The Berenstain Bears' Dollars and Sense (2001)*

The biblical proposition that the love of money is the root of all evil may be arguable. What is not arguable is that kids and money are the root of a lot of aggravation, misery, and table pounding.

### Age zero to one

Though baby Billy is bright as a penny, money—along with dust bunnies, dead bugs, and dog doo—is just something he wants to put in his mouth.

### Age two to three

Though little Billy is fascinated with money and anything bright and shiny, money must remain a spectator sport for him. Just watch as Gramps performs the elbow coin trick or spins a quarter on its edge.

### Age four to five

Billy is ready for Junior Economics 101. He is now capable of understanding that money is a medium of exchange. Of course, in today's run-your-credit-card-through-a-slot culture, the idea of money for goods may be a difficult concept to demonstrate.

However, there are still occasions when Junior can observe the act of

buying something for money. Purchasing a cherry-almond ice cream on a stick from the Good Humor Bear—er, Man—is one such.

## Age six to eight

It is during this period that Junior is likely to raise the subject of an allowance. As in "Daddy, you know my friend Bobby. Well, he gets an allowance. It's five dollars a week [ouch!] and he can spend it on anything he wants."

You have a number of options at this point. You can take the quasi-philosophical position that Junior is too young for an allowance and you don't believe in them anyway. You can pound the table and shout, "Do you think money grows on trees?" You can plead poverty and say, "Daddy's a little short right now. Can we talk about it next week?"

Or you can go along with the general trend and grant Junior an allowance of however much you think is appropriate.

You might also want to introduce the idea of money for work and require Junior to earn his allowance by doing some simple chore like cleaning out the spittoons.

**Age nine to twelve**

Now that Junior has a regular allowance, it's time to begin instructing him in the rudiments of money management. During this period, the problem of overspending and the issue of advances on next week's allowance are likely to come up. This is an excellent opportunity for Dad to teach Junior an important lesson: what it's like to be broke. How to resolve the family conflict that flares up when Mom presses Dad to give tearful Junior an advance on next week's allowance is largely a matter of individual family style.

**Age thirteen to seventeen**

During this period when Junior is reaching out to the world, there will be ample opportunity for him to learn about some of the intricacies of finance. There's budgeting, for example.

"Now, let me see if I understand this, Junior. You've blown your whole allowance on a share of a used guitar with three other guys?"

Dipping into capital is another important concept.

"No, you may not take money out of your bank account. That's birthday and Christmas money Gramps and Gran gave you for college, and under no circumstances . . ."

Having built a firm foundation for Junior's financial future, we move to the next and last stage.

## Age eighteen and beyond

Eureka and hallelujah! Junior is off to college! Of course, Punxsutawney State wasn't his first choice and he's not quite sure what he wants to do. But that's okay. It takes a kid a while to find himself these days—and Mom and Dad aren't looking forward to being empty nesters anyway.

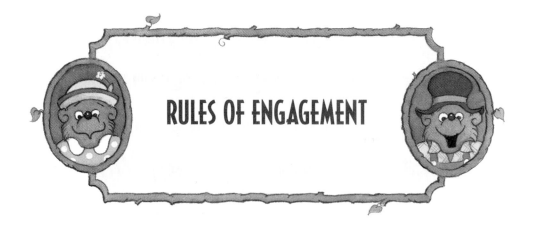

# RULES OF ENGAGEMENT

*It was a lazy sort of day in Bear Country. The air was so still that the leaves on the big tree house where the Bear family lived were hardly rustling.*

*Except in the beehive, where the bees were always busy, nothing much seemed to be happening.*

*It was the sort of day that sometimes leads to mischief.*

*Inside the tree house Brother and Sister Bear were sitting around not doing anything in particular.*

*Brother was holding his soccer ball—he'd become interested in soccer and had been outside practicing free kicks. Sister was relaxing in an easy chair, thinking about what to do next.*

*Neither Papa nor Mama Bear was around. Papa was in his shop working on some furniture, and Mama was out shopping.*

*"My goodness!" complained Sister. "You don't want to do <u>anything</u>. All you want to do is sit there and hug that soccer ball. I think you must be in love with that soccer ball!"*

*"I am not!" protested Brother. "But I'll tell you something—I bet I can dribble this ball past you!"*

*Brother was a pretty good soccer player and a <u>very</u> good dribbler. But so was Sister.*

*The only one who saw what happened next, besides the cubs, was a mockingbird who was perched on a twig outside an open window.*

*Brother faced Sister. The ball was on the floor between them. First Brother moved the ball with his right foot, then with his left, trying to trick Sister out of position.*

*Then, quick as a flash, he gave the ball a sharp kick with his right.*

*It almost worked.*

*But Sister was fast too. She reached out with her knee and blocked the ball, which bounced against a bookshelf, against a chair, against a footstool, and into Mama's <u>most favorite</u> lamp, which fell to the floor with a crash!*

*The mockingbird let out a screech and got out of there as fast as its wings could carry it. As it flew away it saw Mama Bear returning from the marketplace!*

*Now, the Bear family had some house rules just as any family has. One was "No honey eating in bed." Another was "No tracking mud on the clean floors." And another was "<u>No ball playing in the house</u>"!*

FROM *The Berenstain Bears and the Truth* (1983)

A set of enforceable rules is as necessary to the proper conduct of a home as a body of laws is to the proper conduct of the government. But until a child is about two years old, he or she can't really grasp anything so abstract and amorphous as a rule. Until Junior reaches the age of two, he or she is, in effect, the embodiment of his five senses: sight, hearing, touch, taste, and smell.

Training a very young child is like training a clever dachshund, except that it's more difficult. The dachshund's natural instinct is to please. Junior's natural instinct is to hide under the sofa, or take off all his clothes and run down the street naked, or try to flush the cat down the toilet.

In the early stages, establishing a set of household rules is largely a matter of physical control.

If, for example, Junior tries to climb onto the sofa (from which he will almost certainly take a painful tumble), say "no" in a firm, friendly manner, remove him from the site, and distract him with a favorite toy.

Any show of anger or frustration or loud repetitions of the word *no* will be counterproductive. Junior will learn to say "no" soon enough without any help from you.

Patience, repetition, and distraction are musts when trying to set rules for very young children.

If you should begin to lose patience after removing Junior from the sofa for the fourth time, it may help to try to look at the situation from his point of view. Here's how it might look through his eyes:

*Uh-oh, here they come again! . . . What could these great hulking creatures possibly want from me? . . .*

66

*They pick me up. . . . They put me down. . . . Whatever I want to do, they want me to do something else. . . . <u>What is their problem</u>?*

Eventually Junior will "get it." He will come to understand in some small way that he is involved in a mutually beneficial relationship. He may even accept the hitherto unacceptable idea of boundaries.

Turning your little anarchist into a solid citizen is a long-term project. It will take the persistence, endurance, and inner strength that come with knowing you have no choice but to succeed.

Here are some thoughts and ideas that may help.

## Keep rules simple

Since the enforceability of rules varies inversely with their complexity, simplicity should be your goal. *"Don't . . . jump . . . on . . . the . . . bed!!!,"* for example, is much better than "Please, sweetie, Mommy would much rather you didn't jump on the bed. It's dangerous and you might get hurt and then Mommy would be sad."

There is always the option of building the punishment into the rule, as in "Don't jump on the bed or there'll be no TV tonight." But that, as in so many things in life, is a matter of personal style.

## The fewer the better

A small number of tightly written rules is infinitely easier to enforce than a multiplicity of the same. The traffic code, for example, which fits into that little book they give you when you take your driving test, is an administrative piece of cake compared with the tax code, which fills a whole library.

## Accentuate the negative

Negatively stated rules are more effective than positively stated ones. *"Don't . . . go . . . in . . . the . . . street!!!,"* for example, is more memorable and persuasive than "Please play in the driveway where it's safe, sweetie." Also avoid modifications and exceptions, such as "Please play in the driveway, sweetie, *unless Mommy or Daddy is watching."*

It is important, however, not to overdramatize your directives lest you create what lawyers call "an attractive hazard."

### The credibility factor

Since nothing is more delicate and crumbly than parental credibility, don't lay down any rules you are not prepared to enforce. Thus, "If you don't pick up this stuff, I'm going to throw it in the trash" is unlikely to be effective because any three-year-old worth his materialistic salt knows you're not going to throw away $79 worth of LEGOs. Whereas, "If you don't pick up this stuff, I'm going to put it up in the attic for a month!" might be persuasive.

### To spank or not to spank

The old premonitory wheeze "This is going to hurt you more than it's going to hurt me" is truer than the parent who opines it knows. What spanking and other forms of physical punishment may hurt is the bond of love and trust between parent and child.

Here's something else to bear in mind: the child may eventually grow bigger and stronger than the parent, and backsides never forget.

There are more than enough effective punishments available when needed without resorting to spanking, hitting, and smacking. They range from time-outs and suspension of privileges to early curfew and grounding when the child grows older.

## Looking ahead

It is easy enough to manage and control your child when he or she is young. But what's to keep your youngster on the right track when he or she is no longer under your eye and thumb at middle and high school, and eventually at college? Ultimately the only hold we have over our adult children is their need for our admiration and love. We are talking about heartstrings, not apron strings—the cord of trust—the mystical umbilical that forever ties us to our children, and them to us.

So keep an even strain. Try not to lose your temper more than once a week and you may reach the point where your young adult son or daughter looks in the mirror and decides that, all things considered, you've done a pretty good job of parenting.

# RAISING A READER

*Brother and Sister Bear liked books and reading. Mama Bear encouraged them to go to the library often. They took out lots of books.*

*Sister and Brother Bear were at the Bear Country Library. Sister had already chosen her books and was waiting at the checkout desk.*

*"Brother Bear," said Sister impatiently, "are you going to take all day to pick your books?"*

*"Hold your horses," said Brother. "I'm looking for a good mystery."*

*Sister Bear usually took out storybooks and books about nature—and sometimes books of poems. Brother liked those, too, but lately he'd become interested in mysteries—especially spooky ones.*

*"Hey, this one looks good," he said finally. "Okay, let's check out."*

FROM *The Berenstain Bears in the Dark (1982)*

There is nothing better we can do for our children—after fulfilling our obligations to feed, clothe, shelter, and love them—than to put them on the richly rewarding road to books and reading: the road where they will have the opportunity to go through the looking glass with Alice, mess about in boats with Ratty and Mr. Toad, visit the land of Brobdingnag with Gulliver, find their way into the Secret Garden, and go fishing in McElligot's Pool with Dr. Seuss.

Nor has the advent of that remarkable phenomenon the World Wide Web diminished the importance of reading. Quite the contrary: for what is the World Wide Web but a vast, nearly limitless electronic book?

There is also the economic value of reading to consider. For unless you are the second coming of Tiger Woods's dad, there is nothing better you can do to enhance your youngster's future earning power than to encourage him or her to be a reader.

Here are some thoughts, ideas, and suggestions on what you can do to start your child on this journey.

**Read to your baby**

At the outset of our joint career as writers/illustrators of children's books, we were very fortunate in our choice of editor—or, more accurately, his choice of us. Our first editor was Theodor Geisel, aka Dr. Seuss.

When Ted became our editor, he had just come off the triumph of *The Cat in the Hat,* the first of his revolutionary easy-to-read books for kids. *The Cat* led to Beginner Books, a series of books designed to help and encourage kids to read. Ted was so dedicated to getting kids to read that he followed up Beginner Books with Bright and Early Books "for Beginning Beginners," a series for even younger readers. Ted wanted to bring us and our Bears into his new series. We were meeting with him in his eagle's-aerie office in New York. He was frowning over our first fumbling try at a Bright and Early Book.

"It's not simple enough," he said. "It's got to be simpler, easier, younger!"

"How young do you think we can go?" we asked.

He looked at us out of the corner of an eagle eye and said in a faux confidential tone, "Next comes prenatal books. That's right, we're going to project 'em on the wall of the womb!"

We got the idea and created *Inside, Outside, Upside Down,* a book that children as young as eighteen months can enjoy.

Along the same line of thought, we have received more than a few letters from pregnant moms-to-be telling us that they're reading our books to their tummies.

It's a lovely idea. But we'll leave the question of the efficacy of reading to your tummy to the members of the American College of Obstetricians and Gynecologists.

We do believe that reading to your baby from about six months of age on can benefit both Baby and Mom. Baby will enjoy the warmth of Mom's lap and the sound of her voice intoning the words as she turns the pages. Baby may even begin to get the idea that words and objects have something to do with each other.

It's good for Mom because reading to your baby is easier than crawling around on the floor playing choo-choo.

Not that we're letting Daddy off the hook. Baby may well prefer his deep, resonant chest tones to Mom's more dulcet ones.

What kinds of books should you read to your baby? Very simple books. There are lots available that are ideal for the purpose: sturdy board books with one word and one picture on a page. The read-to-your-baby technique is simplicity itself. Mom (or Dad) points to the picture and says "ball," then turns the page and says "cat," and so on.

If all this heavy thinking tires Baby, give your little teether the book and let him gum it for a while.

## Bedtime is story time

There's no better way to build books and reading into your child's life than to establish a regular bedtime story ritual.

A warm, cozy session with *Goodnight Moon, Pat the Bunny,* or *The Very Hungry Caterpillar,* or even *Inside, Outside, Upside Down* (plug!), can be the best part of the day. You may wish to let Junior choose the book of

the evening. The risk in doing so is that he may choose *Curious George Goes to the Hospital* fourteen nights in a row.

Be forewarned also that you edit *Curious George* at your own risk. One skipped phrase will elicit an angry protest. "You left out the part where Curious George steals all the bandages!"

An apologetic "Oops!" may suffice for the offense. Just don't do it again.

It may also happen that Daddy's soporific tones will put *him* to sleep instead of Junior, who now has the option of pounding on Daddy and shouting, "READ! READ!" Or figuring that Daddy needs the sleep more than he does, Junior may slip quietly off Daddy's lap and have a last go with his LEGOs.

**Welcome to Mother Goose Land**

Mother Goose, the Brothers Grimm, and Hans Christian Andersen are just waiting to entertain and enthrall your budding reader. All sorts of exciting things happen in classic children's literature. Little pigs leave home, build houses of variously suitable materials, and run afoul of huffing-and-puffing wolves. Certain individuals put in thumbs and pull out plums. Foolish fellows act upon the notion that they can buy pies with nary a penny. Daredevils risk a hot foot by leaping over flames.

It's a mad, mad world filled with excitement, conflict, suspense, and charismatic characters. The likes of Simon being simple, Jack being nimble, and Little Boy Blue falling asleep on the job are powerful stuff for little kids, as fully capable of entering their lives as a Shakespeare sonnet or Cole Porter song is of entering the lives of adults.

As your young reader encounters a wider range of authors at school, libraries, and bookstores, an array of modern classics presents itself. Books and reading tend to spill over into imaginative activity and play. Purple crayons are as available to readers as they are to Crockett Johnson's Harold. Maurice Sendak's *Where the Wild Things Are* permits children to imagine their own "wild things." Angelina Ballerina may be a mere mouse, but she has inspired many a pirouette on the part of her readers.

**Books and reading versus everything else**

Why do educators, librarians, and people like us make such a fuss about books and reading? Why do we claim that books and reading are more beneficial to children than television, movies, and videos?

What can books and reading do for a youngster that these admittedly more powerful media cannot?

Books and reading enhance, encourage, and nourish the invaluable faculty of imagination. Consider, for example, Robert Louis Stevenson's *Treasure Island* and the situation its hero, Jim Hawkins, finds himself in: separated from his friends on the *Hispaniola* in the West Indies, he is thrown together with that most piratical of pirates Long John Silver. The young reader can't help but imagine him- or herself in Jim's situation, can't help but empathize (without imagination there can be no empathy) with Jim's quandary as he confronts the contradictions of Long John Silver's personality—the old cutthroat appears to be evil personified, but he is protective and kindly toward Jim.

Or what do you do if you're Jack and have to decide whether to trade your fatherless family's last cow for a handful of unprepossessing beans—or you're Hansel or Gretel with a sweet tooth as big as the Ritz and you come to a candy cottage presided over by a witch who makes the Wicked Witch of the West look like Betty Crocker?

The nature of books and reading fosters such imaginings and provides ample opportunity to stop and think, to consider options, to imagine the appearance of characters and settings, to empathize with Jim, Jack, and Hansel and Gretel.

Not so television, movies, and videos. All they provide is the opportunity to sit and be overwhelmed by the headlong power of moving images, pounding sounds, and surging music. Imagination need not apply. All the imagining has been done for you. All the young viewer needs to supply is eyeballs and a vacant stare.

Do all books encourage and nourish the imagination? Since it is the nature of books and reading, not the quality of the books, in question, the answer is probably yes—which raises the related questions of what kind of books your children should read and how to encourage them to do so.

**Let your kids pick their own books**

While it is perfectly permissible and advisable for parents to gently urge their children in the direction of "good books," the last thing a youngster needs at a time when he or she is beginning to feel some sense of autonomy is to be told which friends to choose, what clothes to wear, what music to listen to—and what books to read.

Of course you want your child to be exposed to the classics, to appreciate fine literature. But don't fret if his or her taste runs to popular series like Tales from the Crypt or the latest book on snowboarding. The important thing is that your child is reading!

So whatever sort of reading habit your child develops, encourage and support it! Hey, you grew up on Sweet Valley High, Teenage Mutant Ninja Turtles, and the jokes that came on bubblegum wrappers, and look how wonderfully cultured and classy you turned out.

# STRANGER DANGER

"How was everything at the village green?" asked Mama on the way home in the car. Sister sat in the front with Mama, and Brother rode in the back with the barrel of apples.

"All right, I guess," said Sister. "But there were so many strangers!"

Later at home, when Mama and Sister were getting ready to make applesauce, Mama said, "You know, what Papa told you was quite right. It's <u>not</u> a good idea to talk to strangers or accept presents or rides from them."

"But," she continued, "<u>that doesn't mean that all strangers are bad</u>. Why, chances are, there wasn't a single person on that green that would harm a fly, much less a fine little cub like you. The trouble is . . . well, it's like this barrel of apples. There's an old saying that goes, 'There'll always be a couple of bad apples in every barrel.' That's the way it is with strangers. Cubs have to be careful because of a few 'bad apples.'"

"Look!" said Sister. "I found one! It's all bumpy and has a funny shape."

*"Well, it certainly is strange-looking," said Mama. "But that doesn't necessarily mean it's bad. You can't always tell from the outside which are the 'bad apples.'"*

*She cut it in half.*

*"See?" she said. "It's fine inside."*

*"Now here's one that looks fine on the outside—but inside, it's all wormy."*

*"Yugh!" said Sister.*

FROM *The Berenstain Bears Learn About Strangers (1985)*

Of all the thousands of images and episodes we have created for our Berenstain Bears book series, the "wormy apple" episode has elicited the greatest response. We have received hundreds of letters from parents thanking us for

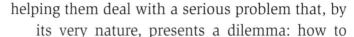

helping them deal with a serious problem that, by its very nature, presents a dilemma: how to arm children against "stranger danger" without turning them into timorous little beasties afraid of their own shadows?

It's not surprising, given the depth of parents' fears, that a minor industry devoted to child safety has sprung up in the dark interstices of our culture. Cautionary lectures by friendly police officers have become as routine in school assemblies as the Pledge of Allegiance. More tots have learned to dial 911 than have learned to recite "Mary Had a Little Lamb." You can get your youngster fingerprinted in the child-identity trailer in the supermarket parking lot. And there are dozens of Web sites offering handy-dandy "identi-kid" kits, complete with a special vial for a DNA sample.

Without for a moment minimizing the value of such measures, we shall concentrate on prevention, an ounce of which is worth its weight in gold. Granted, however, that is a difficult subject with all kinds of implications that four-year-old Billy isn't quite ready for.

When *do* you talk to your kids about stranger danger, and how do you bring up the subject? Windy lectures out of the clear blue sky usually don't mean much to very young children. You are far likelier to get through to them if the subject arises from the loam of ordinary, everyday events, as in "Why do I have to hold your hand at the mall, Mommy?" or "Why can't I walk to Bobby's house by myself?" or "Why do you have to walk me to the school-bus stop? It makes me look like a baby to the other kids."

Any one of the above questions and the dozens of similar ones that come up every day offer ample opportunity for introducing the subject. The specifics of your presentation are up to you. Notwithstanding all the advice from books available (including this one), you know your child better than anyone else.

But however you approach it, it's important to talk about the subject as soon as your child is out and about—as important, for example, as teaching him or her not to run into the street. The danger represented by onrushing vehicles is easy for even the youngest child to understand: you run into the street and you get squashed flatter than Flat Stanley, the two-dimensional hero of a series of children's books.

The danger represented by strangers is darker and more complicated. It has to do with that sinister imponderable, "the evil that lurks in the hearts of men," to quote from *The Shadow* of early radio fame—hardly a subject you'd want to raise with a four-year-old.

But stranger danger is real, and somehow its nature has to be gotten across to kids without giving them nightmares. The last thing you want to do is make the idea of strangers so scary that your child sees the whole world as a Grand Guignol of monsters. Mama Bear's "apple barrel" approach is one reassuring way of making the case that though some strangers may be wicked and dangerous, they are few and far between.

Kids know about wicked. The woods of classic children's tales are well stocked with wickedness. There's the wicked witch who puts Sleeping Beauty into a very sound sleep, the candy-cottage witch who plans to snack on Hansel and Gretel, and a whole assortment of wicked stepsisters, giants, and dragons. However, the classic tale that is best suited for the purpose of instructing your youngster about being wary of strangers is the story of Little Red Riding Hood. Here's how you might enlist Red Riding Hood's wolf in the cause. You've just finished reading "Little Red Riding Hood" to four-year-old Billy. The woodsman who came to Red Riding Hood's rescue has just cut open the wolf and found Granny inside. Billy is sitting there hugging his knees with satisfaction at the wolf's grisly demise.

"Wow!" says Mom. "That was some story!"

No comment from Billy, who is still grooving on the denouement.

"You know," continues Mom, "I don't think it was such a good idea for Little Red Riding Hood to be friendly with that dangerous, wicked wolf."

Billy cocks an eye at Mom, sensing that she's got something on her mind.

"Of course," Mom continues, "there aren't any dangerous, wicked wolves around anymore, but there are some dangerous, wicked people. . . ."

How you proceed from there is up to you. To a great extent it depends on the nature of your child. If your youngster is naturally wary and cautious, Little Red Riding Hood's wolf might suffice. But, on the other hand, if your youngster is a super-friendly kind of kid who shouts "Hi" to every stranger passing by, you may want to go up a notch to "Hansel and Gretel."

But however you approach the task of cautioning your children about strangers, it's important that you do it in a serious, balanced way—one that suits your child. With very small children, you might need to help them understand what a stranger is. For example, a stranger is someone you and they haven't met before. Give a concrete example of who you would consider a stranger.

Many children will pursue the subject with questions—difficult questions—such as "Why are there wicked people?" and "What do they do to children?" You've got no choice but to answer them as best you can—in a generalized, age-appropriate way, of course. There's plenty of time for lurid details later, when your kids will probably know more about the subject than you do.

In today's world, even very young children know that bad things happen. Fights break out. People get shot. Things blow up. With very young children, characterizing stranger danger as just part of the way things are will probably suffice.

The last page of our book *The Berenstain Bears Learn About Strangers* carries a list titled "Brother and Sister Bear's Rules for Cubs." Of the hundreds of letters we have received from parents telling us that our book has helped them deal with the very difficult subject of stranger danger, there have been dozens that told us of specific incidents in which our list helped their children avoid danger. The incidents have ranged from scary to hair-raising.

In one dreadful case, a letter from the mother of a nine-year-old girl told us that her daughter had been molested, but the girl had been afraid to report the incident because the molester, a neighbor, had said he would kill her parents if she told. It wasn't until months after, when the mother and daughter came to the last page of our book, the one with the list, that the girl said, "That happened to me, Mommy." The police were called, the facts were verified, and the neighbor was convicted and is now in prison.

We are deeply grateful for such letters from parents. It's one thing to try to be helpful by writing little picture books about a bear family who lives down a sunny dirt road deep in Bear Country. It's quite another to hear that they have helped kids and parents in ways small and large.

Herewith an expanded version of the list that appears in our book. You may want to share it with your children.

**BROTHER AND SISTER BEAR'S RULES FOR CUBS**

1. Don't talk to strangers. Most strangers are nice, but as Mama Bear says, there are almost always a couple of bad apples in the barrel. And since you can't always tell the good ones from the bad ones, it's best not to talk to strangers.

2. Never take candy or other gifts from a stranger. Grown-ups know that they're not supposed to offer candy or other gifts to children they don't know. So if a stranger offers you candy—even if it's your favorite kind—get away from him (it will usually be a "him," though not always) as fast as you can and tell a teacher, crossing guard, or police officer if one is nearby.

3. Never go anywhere with a stranger—and especially don't get into a car with a stranger. No matter what they say, do not go with them. Not even if they say, "Your mommy has been hurt and she wants me to take you to her," or "I have lost my puppy (or kitten). Would you please help me look for it?" Whatever they say, do not go with them. Don't let them get close to you. Run away if you have to, or run into a nearby store; or holler to the mailman across the street, or the gas-station man down the block.

4. Don't wander off by yourself. Whether you are at the supermarket or the mall, at a movie or a museum, stay close to your mom or dad or other grown-up who brought you. If you are going to the playground on Saturday or walking home from the school-bus stop, do it with friends. There is safety in numbers.

5. Don't keep secrets from your parents—especially if someone asks you to. Anyone who asks you to keep secrets from your parents means you harm.

Your parents love you. They will protect you from anyone who threatens them or you. If anything like that happens, tell your parents about it right away. They'll know what to do.

6. Your body is your personal property and nobody else's business—especially the private parts. If anyone, whether it's a stranger or even someone you know, tries to touch you there, get away from that person as quickly as you can and tell your parents about it. Again, they'll know what to do.

7. You can't have rules for everything, so use your common sense. Common sense is what helps us by telling us what to do in situations that are not covered by rules.

Like so many parenting concerns, the problem of stranger danger presents a contradiction: it requires constant vigilance and close supervision of your child's comings and goings—and, at the same time, an understanding that your youngster needs to develop a sense of autonomy and trust as he or she grows older. But it can be managed. Just apply rule seven from the list.

# WEIGHING IN ON OBESITY

*Bear Country, where the Bear family lived in the big tree house down a sunny dirt road, was a happy, healthy place.*

*There were lots of cozy nooks and comfortable trees for the Bear Country folk to live in. The weather was good most of the time. And best of all, there was plenty of good, healthy food—worms and seeds for the birds, nuts and acorns for the squirrels, grass and dandelions for the rabbits, more than enough flies for the frogs, and plenty of good, nourishing food for the Bears: honey, of course, but more important, lots of fruits, vegetables, milk, fish, and fowl.*

*The trouble was that certain bears had gotten into the habit of eating not-so-healthy foods when watching TV, at the movies, and at the mall.*

*In fact, it began to seem to Mama Bear that anytime was snack time.*

*At first she hadn't paid much attention, but then one day when the cubs were raiding the pantry, Mama noticed something. The cubs were getting a little chubby. She took a closer look just to be sure.*

Yes, they were chubbier from the side. They were chubbier from the front. They were chubbier from the back.

There was no question about it. Brother and Sister were going to have to stop eating all that junk food!

"But, Mama," they protested. "We're growing bears and we need those snacks!"

"You're growing, all right," said Mama. "The trouble is you're growing from side to side as much as you are up and down! Sometimes cubs get into bad habits, and you've gotten into the habit of eating altogether too many sweets and goodies. We're going to have to get back to healthy, nourishing food!" She gathered up all the goodies in one big load.

"Mama!" cried Sister Bear. "What are you doing?"

"You're not going to throw them away?" cried Brother.

"No, we're going to put them in the freezer and forget about them," she said. "And there's no use arguing!"

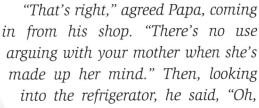

"That's right," agreed Papa, coming in from his shop. "There's no use arguing with your mother when she's made up her mind." Then, looking into the refrigerator, he said, "Oh, dear! We're out of Sweetsie-Cola. Let's be sure to get some next time we're at the supermarket."

"Our Sweetsie-Cola days are over," said Mama. As she pushed all the goodies into the freezer, two packages fell to the floor.

"Say!" shouted Papa. "What are you doing with my Sugar Balls and Choco-Chums?"

*"They're going into the freezer and we're going to forget about them!" cried Brother. "We're going to eat healthy, nourishing food instead."*

*"Just a minute!" said Papa. But as he leaned over to pick up his precious goodies, there was a loud r-r-r-i-p! Papa's snack habits had caught up with him, too. He had split the seat of his overalls wide open.*

FROM *The Berenstain Bears and Too Much Junk Food (1985)*

The problem of juvenile obesity is bulging to a crisis. Surveys have shown that lack of exercise coupled with unhealthy eating habits has caused an epidemic of juvenile obesity.

But what to do about it?

You could join a class-action suit against the Amalgamated Fast Food Emporia of the Universe, or you can take direct action by employing some simple commonsense measures to work on the problem.

Here are twenty ways to decrease your youngster's caloric intake while increasing his or her energy output.

1. Set a good example. You don't have to do anything drastic like going on the John Carradine Diet.* Just cut back on desserts and everything else you like.

2. About five times a day, think of something you forgot to bring downstairs and send Junior upstairs to get it.

3. Hide the remote.

4. Blast all fast-food joints with your invisible ray gun.

---

*Unlike most celebrity diets, the John Carradine Diet is simplicity itself: just stop eating until you look like John Carradine.

5. Buy your youngster a butterfly net and pay a dime for every butterfly he or she brings back alive.

6. Declare your entire house a salty-snack-free zone.

7. Encourage your kid to go out for a team—*any* team.

8. Prohibit all TV channels except for PBS.

9. Switch from whole milk to skim milk.

10. Switch from ice cream to sorbet.

11. Encourage Junior to take up the sousaphone and go out for marching band.

12. Jog to church (or anywhere).

13. Switch from sorbet to Jell-O.

14. Donate your TV to the town dump.

15. Encourage your teenager to volunteer at the hospital. Hospital food being what it is, your youngster is likely to reduce food intake and, volunteer duties being what they are, he or she is likely to increase energy output. Hospital service also looks good on college applications.

16. Supply your youngster with a pedometer and pay 50¢ a mile with the stipulation that the money may not be spent on edibles.

17. March for a good cause.

18. Wean your youngster away from passé soda to fashionable imported bottled water.

19. Declare your house a candy-free zone—except perhaps for the little Valentine's Day candy hearts that say "I Love You," jellybeans on Easter, and candy canes on Christmas.

20. Put a scale next to the fridge.

# COUNTERING PEER PRESSURE

"Hey! Wait a minute!" said Too-Tall. "I might be able to use a cub like you. You've got moxie."

"Moxie?" said Brother.

"Yeah. Spunk. Nerve. Moxie." He put a big arm around Brother's shoulders. "Why don't you come with us and have a little fun?"

The rest of the gang gathered around and Brother said, "I really think I better be go—"

"Whatsa matter?" said one. "Chicken?"

Another one began strutting, flapping his arms like a chicken, and clucking, "Puk, puk, puk—_aaw_! Puk, puk, puk—_aaw_!" Pretty soon the whole gang was strutting and clucking all over the place.

"I am not chicken!" protested Brother.

"Prove it," said Too-Tall. "Come along with us for some fun."

Brother was a little nervous about joining the gang, but he certainly didn't want them to think he was chicken. So when they scampered off into the woods, he followed.

He got more and more nervous as they led him along the

*dangerous old quarry path, across Roaring Creek, and past the Spooky Old Tree.*

*After a few more twists and turns, Too-Tall signaled a stop. When Brother saw where they were, he was surprised and pleased.*

*"Hey!" he said. "This is Farmer Ben's watermelon pa—"*

*"Shhh!" hissed Too-Tall, clapping a hand over his mouth. "You want to spoil our fun?"*

*It turned out that Too-Tall's idea of fun was to run off with one of Farmer Ben's watermelons. And as the newest member of the gang, Brother was the one expected to do it.*

*"But Farmer Ben is a friend of mine," he protested. "And besides, it isn't honest!"*

*The gang flapped their arms like chickens and clucked, "Puk, puk, puk—aaw!" into Brother's ear.*

*"I'm not chicken!" Brother insisted.*

*"Then go ahead and take the watermelon," said Too-Tall. "Farmer Ben'll never miss it."*

*Brother Bear looked all around. Ben was nowhere to be seen and it was sort of exciting being in the gang.*

*"Dare you," said Too-Tall. Brother didn't move.*

*"Double-dare you!" said the gang. Brother still didn't move.*

*"Dee-double-dare you!" said Too-Tall and the gang.*

*The dee-double-dare did it. Ever so quietly, ever so carefully, Brother Bear crept through the tall grass, through the fence, and past the* NO TRESPASSING, PRIVATE PROPERTY *sign and picked out the biggest, fattest, greenest watermelon in the patch. Then he broke off the stem, picked it up, and—*

*"Gotcha! You thievin' varmint!" shouted a voice.*

FROM *The Berenstain Bears and the Double Dare (1988)*

The bad news about peer pressure and its consequences makes the news every day. The datelines cover just about every city, town, and wide place in the road in the United States. The headlines cover just about every imaginable kind of peer-pressure-driven risky behavior—from drug use to underage smoking and drinking, from teen sex to vandalism.

On a bad day, it looks like a beered-up, drug-ridden, chain-smoking, sex-mad teen jungle out there.

But teens don't come from outer space or materialize from the ether. They start out as little children, our own darling little girls and boys. That's when to start teaching them about peer pressure. They will encounter it, as surely as the night follows the day, as soon as they begin interacting with their little friends.

As in the following example, for instance: Four-year-old Billy has come home looking for all the world as if he has been rolling around in mud. "Good grief!" cries Mother. "What's happened to you? However did you get into such a dreadful condition?"

"Well," says Billy, "the other kids were rolling in the mud, so I had to do it, too."

It's tempting in such a situation to jump up and down and scream, "Don't you have a mind of your own?" or "If the other kids jumped off a cliff, would you do it, too?"

Since the answers to those questions may well be "no" and "yes," it's best not to go there.

A better idea is to begin preparing your youngster for what lies ahead. Your approach might go something like this: "You know, sweetie, sometimes your friends might want you to do something you shouldn't. Why, I remember one time when I was a little girl, my friend Charlene . . ."

"You mean like yesterday when I was playing in Herbie's sandbox and he dared me to eat sand?"

"That's exactly what I mean. What happened?"

"It didn't taste good, so I spit it out."

It's a good idea to warn Junior about the dare, the double-dare, and, yes, the dee-double-dare up front (it was the dee-double-dare that goaded straight-arrow Brother Bear into doing the unthinkable: stealing a watermelon from Farmer Ben's melon patch).

Then there's the ultimate peer-pressure weapon, the cry of "chicken!"

It resounds down through the ages. Who knows that it wasn't the cry of "chicken!" that made George Washington chop down the cherry tree or caused Lord Byron to swim the Hellespont?

Instead of remonstrating with Junior for acceding to peer pressure, arm him against it with some pithy responses like "I don't take dares. It's dumb!" or "It takes one to know one!"

Many are the kids who've gotten into trouble for the simple lack of something to say.

At this early stage, peer pressure usually involves the likes of rolling in the mud and eating sand.

The peer-pressure plot thickens a bit when Junior goes off to school.

Junior is unlikely to get into any serious peer-pressure trouble in the beginning of his school career. But don't be too surprised if come third grade, you are called in to school to discuss spitball throwing or Junior's involvement with the group that mooned the ballet club.

When the time comes to impose punishment for such escapades, it may be useful to include peer pressure in your bill of particulars. "Son, I want you to understand that your mother and I are grounding you not so much for what you did, but for letting your idiot friends talk you into it."

Managing the effect of peer pressure becomes more challenging at the middle and high school stages. Much of the problematic behavior of teens is driven by their need for acceptance coupled with a need to declare independence from their parents. These twin needs tend to express themselves through such bizarre behavior as black lipstick, blue hair, and weird clothes.

But before Daddy (it's usually Daddy) goes into outrage mode, he might want to flash back to the funny clothes he wore as a teen.

It's also good to remember that this whole troubled-teen period is complicated by the mad rush of hormones designed to encourage the further population of the planet. To make the situation even more complicated, it's all happening in the middle of a culture war that makes it difficult to discuss the introduction of an intelligent form of sex education in the schools.

With the promoters of abstinence pledges on one side and the condom dispensers on the other, schools often end up in the awkward position of bringing abstinence in the front door and dispensing condoms out the back door.

Ironically, it is the issue of style that generates the greatest parental fuss.

It's best, however, to grin and bear your teen's fads and fancies and save your parental authority for the triple threat of peer-driven behavior: alcohol, drugs, and sex.

Teenage boys and girls are different in ways that have nothing to do with *la différence*. Sometimes boys can be surly, taciturn, and rebellious; sometimes girls can be voluble, tremulous, and needy.

Girls also have a powerful, not-so-secret weapon—they cry.

Consider lovely Julia, for example. She has come to her parents for permission to have an anklet of butterflies tattooed around her lovely ankle. "It's the latest thing! All the girls are doing it—Madison, Dakota, Nebraska! All of them!"

"Over my dead body!" snarls Daddy.

"But, Daddy! It's so cute and sexy."

"Sexy? *Sexy?*" roars Daddy, turning purple.

"Please, Daddy," says Julia, tears welling in her eyes. "You have that tattoo on your arm."

"Yes," says Daddy, who can't stand to see his daughter cry. "But I was in the Navy and it's an anchor."

"Anchor? Butterfly?" says Julia, sensing an advantage. "I don't know what difference that makes. It sounds like male chauvinism to me!"

Leaving the field to Mom, Dad slinks off to his den, muttering, "I knew we were headed down the wrong road when we let her have her ears pierced."

"Now stop crying, sweetie," says Mom, who knows that the three most important words in any crisis involving teens are *negotiate, negotiate, negotiate.*

"Have you stopped to consider," continues Mom, "that a tattoo is permanent? And there's this, too. I'm sure the butterfly anklet would look nice with your high heels, but wouldn't it clash with your clogs and your Birkenstocks?"

Julia dries her tears and turns pensive. The permanence argument might not carry much weight. But she sees merit in the Birkenstock argument.

"How about this," says Mom, pressing her advantage. "Instead of an anklet, how about one adorable little butterfly on your hip just above the bikini line? And don't worry, I'll tell Daddy about it."

"Oh, Mommy," cries Julia, hugging her mom. "I love you!"

Fade out.

The end.

(Until the next crisis.)

Then there's body piercing, the peer-driven teen practice that drives parents even farther up the wall than tattooing. Body piercing, it happens, offers an advantage over tattooing. The nose, eyebrow, or tongue ring can be removed if by some chance the ring bearer should happen to apply for a job. Though it should be kept in mind that, over time, an increasing proportion of personnel managers may themselves be wearing nose, eyebrow, and tongue rings.

There's a disadvantage to body piercing as well. It should be pointed out to young people who are contemplating having their bodies stigmatized: body-piercing parlors aren't necessarily the most germ-free environments. Nose, eyebrow, and tongue infections are no fun.

But not all things are negotiable. Such peer-driven activities as taking drugs, drinking, or any other behavior that risks your youngsters' health and safety must be dealt with firmly. The smell of pot in Junior's room or the smell of booze on his breath are sure signs of trouble.

Just as no two kids are alike, no two families are alike. How to deal with serious problems like drugs and drinking depends on the particular circumstances and the nature of the family relationship.

Has Junior been a reasonably responsible person until now? If that's the case, a serious heart-to-heart talk with no holds barred may get to the bottom of what's going on. Is Junior hanging with the wrong crowd? Is there a "connection" or a bad influence involved, or is it just a bunch of kids screwing themselves up all by themselves? Maybe the school is part of the problem, notwithstanding all its drug-free-zone signs.

Whatever the underlying problem turns out to be, if the parent-child relationship is loving and on firm ground, the problem can usually be solved. It may be necessary for Junior to find a new set of friends. Even a change of schools may be in order.

If, on the other hand, Junior has had trouble with drugs before, if the parent-child relationship is frayed and you have that awful sinking feeling that you are in over your head, it may be necessary to seek professional help. The school counselor, your family physician, or a trusted clergyperson will have a list of qualified professionals from which to choose. It's a good sign if Junior accepts the idea of counseling. If he resists, Mom and Dad might want to attend a couple of counseling sessions themselves. Who knows? They may be part of the problem.

It's possible.

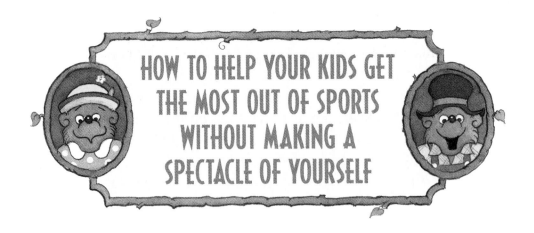

# HOW TO HELP YOUR KIDS GET THE MOST OUT OF SPORTS WITHOUT MAKING A SPECTACLE OF YOURSELF

*As soon as Brother and Sister felt the first warmth of the spring sun, they got out their trusty ball, bat, and gloves and began limbering up for the season.*

*"Seems to me," said Papa, "that you cubs might want to think about playing some real baseball on a real baseball field. It says right here in the paper that the Bear Country Cub League is going to be holding tryouts pretty soon. You might want to sign up."*

*"Now, hold on," interrupted Mama. "That's a high-powered league over there, and those tryouts involve quite a lot of pressure."*

*"Pressure?" asked Sister. "What do you mean?"*

*"You'll be competing against lots of other cubs and not everybody is going to make the team," said Mama. "But you both play pretty well," she added, "so it's up to you."*

*"Won't hurt to drive over and have a look," said Papa.*

*"Wow!" said Brother when he saw the Cub League field. It was a real field with fences and foul lines and real bases and grandstands and everything.*

*And the teams wore uniforms! Brother and Sister signed up right then and there!*

*They got ready for the tryouts by practicing. They practiced fielding and hitting. Mama showed them how to choke up on the bat against fast pitching. They even practiced bunting and base running. But as tryout day drew near, they began to get a little nervous.*

*"Try to calm down," said Mama. "It's only a game. Besides, the worst that can happen is that you won't make the team. You can always try out again next year."*

*"No, that's not the worst that can happen," said Brother, looking gloomy. "The worst that can happen is if Sis makes the team and I don't!"*

*"I consider that a sexist remark!" snapped Sister angrily.*

FROM *The Berenstain Bears Go Out for the Team (1986)*

In the dear dead days not quite beyond recall, kids' sports activities were the province of the kids themselves. They chose up teams for their own back-lot baseball games, and they organized their own two-hand-touch street football games (with ground rules like: the sidewalk and all parked cars are out of bounds; there's an automatic time-out for moving traffic; and if the ball goes into old

Mrs. Krovny's yard, we draw straws to see who goes and gets it). All basket-ball required was an indeterminate number of kids, a ball, and a bushel peach basket with the bottom knocked out nailed to the wall.

Those were the days of "Where did you go?"—"Out."—"What did you do?"—"Nothing." Back then, grown-ups had the grace and good sense to leave kids to their own devices. Not that those unsupervised kids' games were free of pressure, mortification, and bloody noses. Being the last one chosen in a choose-up game, losing a fly ball in the sun, and crossing the wrong goal are a few traumatic experiences that come to mind.

Bloody noses were supplied by the tough kids from across the tracks, who confiscated not only the field but every bat, ball, and glove in sight.

But that was then, and this is now—and, boy, is it ever different!

Now it's the grown-ups who beat up on each other.

Now there's a vast network of adult-sponsored, adult-organized kids' sports leagues from here to Timbuktu and back.

Herewith a tot-to-teen guide on how to help your youngster get the most out of sports without making a spectacle of yourself or unnecessarily damaging his or her psyche.

**The T-ball experience**

T-ball is a form of baseball designed for small children who don't know how to get to first base—or second or third base, for that matter.

Since hitting a round ball with a round bat is generally considered one of the more difficult tasks in sports, T-ballers are not expected to hit a thrown ball. They are charged with hitting a ball set upon a waist-high tee (thus the name T-ball). As often as not, however, the T-baller hits the tee rather than the ball. This makes a satisfying WHACK!

But it is not the object of the game. The object of the game is to hit the ball and then, having hit the ball, run the bases.

Since the average four- to five-year-old is relatively low on the baseball learning curve, a surfeit of coaches is required. T-ball coaches have many duties. They are expected to conduct successful batters around the bases in a counterclockwise direction, keep the boy T-ballers from putting frogs down the backs of the girl T-ballers, and take T-ballers who have gone in their pants to the sidelines for a change of uniform.

But for all its frustrations and chaos, T-ball is both a charming and a useful exercise. It's one of the best spectator sports there are, and it can help a parent decide whether a youngster is ready to go to the next level: the Little League minors.

If, for example, your little outfielder is more interested in chasing a butterfly or watching the clouds go by or turning over second base to look for bugs than catching a ball hit in his or her direction, it's fair to assume that he or she needs more seasoning.

**Going out for Little League**

Let's say Junior has demonstrated that he does know how to get to first base and has decided of his own free will to try out for Little League (that is, without undue influence from his baseball-obsessed dad, whose favorite movies are

*Field of Dreams* and *Bull Durham,* and who is a member of a Rotisserie baseball league[*]).

Baseball Dad watches anxiously from the sidelines as Junior and about eighty other seven- to nine-year-olds are put through their paces—batting, throwing, fielding grounders, and shagging fly balls under the watchful gaze of a bunch of men with clipboards.

Hey, who are these guys?

"Hmm," observes Baseball Dad, a shadow of suspicion crossing his mind. Those guys with the clipboards are dads, and at least some of them are dads of some of the kids trying out. Surely this is an occasion for the sin of favoritism, and it certainly has the appearance of a conflict of interest. A terrible thought crosses Baseball Dad's mind. Suppose Junior doesn't make it! But wait a minute! That kid hitting those hard line drives looks like a girl. It *is* a girl!

Good grief! There are at least four other girls out there! Panic stabs at Baseball Dad. His heart skips a beat. What if . . . what if one of those girls makes it and Junior doesn't? What if *all* those girls make it and Junior doesn't?

But hold on! Hold on! It looks like Junior has made it! At least one of those nice clipboard fellows is patting him on the back.

"That's fine, Junior," says Baseball Dad. "But let's not dally. There's still time to get in a little batting practice before dark."

**How to determine whether your youngster wants to play Little League ball or is just doing it to please you**
• Does he pray for rain on game day?
• Does he look the other way when you complain to his manager that he's not getting enough playing time?

---

*The idea for this fantasy baseball competition was first formulated in a restaurant named La Rotisserie Francaise, thus the name Rotisserie baseball.

• When you suggest there might be time before dinner for a little practice, does he say, "Aw, gee, Dad—I'm learning a new chord on my guitar"?

• Does he look relieved when his team fails to make the play-offs?

• Has he failed to bond with the $129 red-leather baseball glove you bought him for making the team?

• Is he perfectly content to play right field (the least demanding of all nine positions)?

• Does he tend to say, "Who, me?" when the manager sends him into the game?

If the answer to any of the above questions is "yes," you might want to consider letting Junior skip Little League next season and encourage him to spend more time with his guitar.

**Boys and girls not quite together**

Though girls have been made welcome in Little League, it took about ten years of pressure and litigation to make it so.

Girls are fairly well represented at the T-ball level. But they dwindle down to a precious few in the Little League minors, and are even fewer and farther between at the major Little League level. As far as we know, no girl has ever played on a team that has made the Little League World Series.

A number of factors account for this decreasing female participation in Little League baseball. For one thing, most boys, especially incipient jocks, are unenlightened male chauvinists. They are also terrified of girls who can bat, pitch, catch, and run better than they can.

But there are other factors that tend to separate the boys from the girls as they approach the teen years. Boys' greater upper-body strength gives them

an athletic advantage; girls' greater upper-body endowment gives them a very different sort of advantage—the ability to make boys forget about baseball.

Girls' softball leagues are another factor. They have proliferated in the last decade. Girls' softball is a very demanding sport, highlighted by the spectacular underhanded "windmill" style of pitching that is standard in the girls' game.

On those occasions when major league baseball players have been taunted into going to the plate against female champion softball windmillers, they have whiffed as often as not.

Perhaps the biggest factor in leveling the field of sports opportunities for girls is a set of federal regulations called Title IX. Title IX requires that colleges and universities that receive federal money (which means virtually every college or university) offer female students the same athletic opportunities they offer male students. This has reflected back through high school, middle school, and even elementary school, and has created a revolution in young women's participation in sports. Athletic scholarships are being offered to every sort of female phenom, from windmilling pitchers to hard-serving tennis whizzes, from towering basketballers to well-seated horsewomen. Horseback riding, incidentally, has the distinction of being the only internationally sanctioned sport in which boys and girls, men and women, and mares and stallions compete on a completely equal basis.

But whether your youngster is an absolute phenom being scouted by the majors, or someone who enjoys sports but enjoys other things as well, or is a confirmed non-jock, the thing to remember is that it's not about you. It's about your youngster and his or her hopes, dreams, and aspirations.

# THE TROUBLE WITH BULLIES

One day, Mama, Papa, and Brother Bear were busy in the yard when Sister Bear came home crying. Her face was scratched and dirty and her clothes were torn. "What happened to you?" asked Mama.

"Please tell us," said Papa.

Brother couldn't believe how beat-up Sister looked. Her jumper and blouse were torn. Her face and fur were a mess. Even her pink bow was drooping.

"Did you fall?" asked Mama. Sister shook her head no.

"Was there an accident?" asked Papa. Once again she shook her head no.

"I think I can tell you what happened," said Brother. "It looks to me like somebody beat her up."

"Beat her up? That's outrageous!" said Papa.

"Who in the world would beat up a sweet little cub like Sister?" asked Mama.

"A bully might," said Brother.

That's when Sister stopped crying long enough to get some

*words out. "B-B-Brother's right," she sobbed. "A no-good nasty rotten bully beat me up—<u>and for no reason</u>!" Just the thought of it made her so angry that she started to cry all over again.*

FROM *The Berenstain Bears and the Bully (1993)*

Because of the tragic events at Columbine High School in Littleton, Colorado, and so many other communities throughout the nation, bullying and its consequences have come under intense scrutiny. School boards have instituted preventative policies, scholarly studies have been written, and panels of experts have appeared on C-SPAN.

What they have discovered is something most of us have known all along: bullying is one of the most damaging behaviors children are subjected to. It attacks their self-esteem, induces depression, and scars their psyches. Parents know this in their bones. They know it from their own painful childhood memories; they know it from even more painful experiences as parents.

There are few parental experiences more devastating than having your child come home crying and beaten up, the victim of a bully.

Troubling though this experience may be to a parent, there are, unfortunately, no quick-and-easy solutions to the problem. There are strategies that can be applied and measures to be taken, but the trouble with bullies is so highly charged that the

107

problem needs to be approached with great care, wisdom, and trepidation.

A further complication is that bullying is not a gender-neutral problem. The difficulty boys have with bullies is generally different from the problems girls encounter. Not that there is no such thing as a girl bully. The "no-good nasty" intimidator who beats up on Sister in *The Bully* happens to be a girl. But girls tend to gang up socially on their victims rather than physically.

Gender is also a factor in how parents respond to the trouble with bullies. Moms tend to cuddle and comfort little Billy when he comes home beaten up. Dads, on the other hand, tend to exhort Junior to "stop crying like a baby and go out there and give that bully what for—and don't come home until you do!"

The difficulty with Dad's approach is that although there's always a chance (a very small chance) that Junior will be able to give the bully what for, there is a greater likelihood that he will hop a train to Schenectady.

Nor is Mom's "cuddle and comfort" approach necessarily the best way to deal with the problem. Comfort, yes. But a little fact-finding might be in order. You may already know the bully in question. Maybe it's Herbie, Scourge of the Sandbox. Perhaps a frank talk with Herbie's mother would have a salutary effect.

Or if Herbie is a repeat offender, a delegation of the moms of all his victims might be persuasive.

It's important at this early age to do what you can to get your child through what can be a very damaging experience. Since no two situations are exactly alike, it's going to be up to you to choose the most constructive course of action.

But just letting it happen is not an option.

As children grow older, the trouble with bullies becomes more serious—to the point where the problem of kids bringing guns to school has become commonplace.

In today's post-Columbine climate, however, any show of weapons, whether guns, knives, or box cutters, in a school setting is apt to be dealt with summarily—the local SWAT team descends on the school, the culprit is trundled off to the police station, the parents are notified, the school folk breathe a collective sigh of relief and go back to vocabulary lists, book reports, and pop quizzes.

But the bully's ordinary, everyday weapon isn't guns, knives, or box cutters. It is ordinary, everyday fists. Fists and the fear of the pain and humiliation they can inflict are the weapons of choice of the schoolyard bully.

How to arm Junior against bullies who can smell vulnerability the way a pig can sniff out truffles?

One way is to encourage your youngster to develop his musculature—to get stronger. We're not suggesting he begin preparing to run for governor of California. But bullies tend to avoid kids who can chin themselves twenty times and do thirty push-ups. A couple of five-pound dumbbells and a chinning bar that can be installed in any doorway are readily available at the fitness store. They can do wonders in building up Junior's biceps, triceps, and self-confidence.

It's amazing how ten-year-old boys take to doing daily sets of curls and chin-ups. As they grunt and groan through their sequences, they fantasize about what they are going to do to you-know-who.

It often happens, however, that by the time Junior has muscled up, countermeasures are no longer necessary. The schoolyard bully has noted that Junior is no longer a sixty-six-pound weakling and has decided to kick sand on somebody else.

But perhaps the bully situation at Junior's school is more serious than you thought. Junior's new muscles may have been sufficient to discourage a run-of-the-mill bully. But now an uber-bully has appeared and is terrorizing the schoolyard, the corridors, and the boys' room.

If that appears to be what's happening, it's time to take your indignation in hand and go to the principal. The principal may be the sort of responsible person who has already arranged for the bully to be transferred to a school for incorrigibles. On the other hand, he or she may be of that older school that holds to the discredited notion that bullies and bullying are just part of growing up. If that's the case, a whole delegation of parents is in order. And if that doesn't work, a full-scale appeal to the school board, accompanied by threats of lawsuits and police action, will all but certainly have the desired effect.

Another option is to consider enrolling Junior in one of the karate, judo, or kendo schools that fill the yellow pages. Junior might like the idea of earning a brown belt. He might get good at it. A demonstration of board and cement-block smashing in the school assembly will make him virtually bully-proof.

What must be guarded against, however, is that he might get *too* good at it and become a bit of a bully himself.

The trouble with bullies can be considerably more serious at the middle and high school levels, when the "jocks versus nerds" antagonism comes into play. The vast majority of school athletes are decent kids, who stand ready and willing to go to the aid of someone who is being bullied.

But if experience and news headlines are any guide, there is often a jock minority who consider it a duty to torment any classmate whom they regard as different.

They travel in packs and go after their victims with the full kit of juvenile cruelty: ethnic and sexual epithets, physical abuse, extortion, and other practices too disgusting to specify. This is when the trouble with bullies gets truly serious. In most of the more notorious cases, it has developed that the school authorities didn't make an effort to find out what was going on beneath the surface of everyday school life.

Or, more disturbing, they have accepted the notion that bullies and bullying are just part of growing up. Then, one fine day, some kid that nobody paid much attention to shows up with an automatic rifle and blows away the lunchroom.

Encourage your school to include communications skills and conflict resolution in the curriculum as a way of circumventing trouble and creating a climate and a culture in which bullying will not be tolerated. It's a long way from Sandbox Herbie to tragedies the likes of Columbine, but the trouble with bullies is all part of the same dynamic. It behooves us all to search our minds and souls to find the ways and means to prevent the next such tragedy.

# MOMMY, WHAT'S GOD?

*Early one weekend morning, Sister Bear was busy having a tea party with her dolls. She poured the tea into each of the dolls' cups. It was really apple juice. Sister didn't much care for tea. She served cookies, too.*

*"You're welcome, my dears," Sister said, pretending that the dolls had thanked her.*

*"Now," she said, folding her hands, "let's say grace."*

*The Bear family usually said grace before meals. Sometimes they were in such a hurry or so hungry that they forgot . . . especially Papa. But Mama usually reminded them.*

*So, Sister bowed her head, closed her eyes, and said:*

> *Thank you for the world so sweet.*
> *Thank you for the food we eat.*
> *Thank you for the birds that sing.*
> *Thank you, God, for everything.*

*Then Sister drank her juice and ate her cookies. The dolls weren't very hungry, so Sister drank their juice and ate their cookies, too.*

Later, when Sister and Mama were washing up the tea things, Sister grew thoughtful. "Mama," she said, a faraway look in her eyes, "what's God?"

Mama took Sister outside into the garden. It was a beautiful morning. The sun was shining, the birds were singing, and the flowers were all in bloom. "Now, Sister," Mama said as she began weeding her garden, "all you need to remember is that God made everything—the birds, the flowers, the sunshine. They're all God's work—all part of God's Great Plan."

Sister looked around at the wide, beautiful world and thought it over. "You mean," she said, "God made <u>everything</u>—everything in the whole wide world?"

"That's right, dear," said Mama.

"Did He make clouds and trees and butterflies?" asked Sister.

"Of course," answered Mama. "Everything."

But Sister didn't stop there. "Did He make worms and spiders and big yellow slugs?" she asked.

*"Yes," nodded Mama, feeling a little sick as she picked a big yellow slug off her favorite geraniums. "As I said, they're all part of God's Great Plan."*

FROM *The Berenstain Bears and the Big Question (1999)*

Sooner rather than later, your child is going to hear the name of the Deity, either sacramentally from the pulpit or taken in vain when Daddy hits his thumb with a hammer, and ask The Big Question, "Mommy, what's God?"

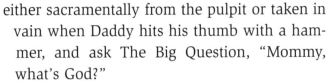

It's an important question, and as with most such questions, there are a number of ways of approaching the answer.

There's always the option of just winging it. But that could lead to your making a stuttering hash of what could be an important moment and an even more important question.

Or you might want to punt and say, "That's a very good question, sweetie. Why don't we wait till the Sabbath and ask Minister Jones (or Rabbi Zuckerman or Imam Abdullah)?"

It's possible, of course, that you studied religion as a second major in college and have a fully formed answer right on the tip of your tongue.

What's more likely, however, is that given the 24/7 demands of contemporary life, you haven't thought about The Big Question since your First Communion, your bat mitzvah, or the time you last attempted to keep the fast during Ramadan. In which case, you'd better think about a couple of things in advance of the question and the moment.

Thing one: Before trying to answer The Big Question for your child, you might want to consider answering it for yourself. Most of us harbor the notion that somewhere deep inside our minds and our souls, we've got a pretty good answer—it's just that we can't quite put it into words. That won't cut it for Junior, who needs to have it put into words—age-appropriate words. We wouldn't presume to tell you how to answer The Big Question. It's up to you to search your convictions and religious tradition for the best answer. We do suggest that as Junior's first teacher, you have a responsibility to take your child's religious inquiries seriously and answer them as best you can.

Thing two: It's a good idea for you and your spouse to have your doctrinal ducks in a row before you begin your child's religious instruction. It won't do for you to tell Junior that "God created the universe and all things therein," only to have Daddy say, God forbid, that "there is no God." That sort of thing can lead anywhere—even to the Supreme Court (as it already has).

Differences in opinion on the religious upbringing of kids tend to be a troublesome marital issue— nor does it take a major disagreement to generate trouble. A simple lack of enthusiasm on the part of one parent can make for a rift.

But just as Sister Bear raised questions about Mama Bear's answer to The Big Question, so will your children. Here are some thoughts, ideas, and suggestions on how you might want to answer some of the stickier ones.

**"Where do we go when we die, Mommy?"**
Kids don't have to worry about taxes, but with goldfish, baby turtles, gerbils, et al. dying around them willy-nilly, they're bound to have intimations of

mortality. It's a great temptation when faced with a tearful child who has just lost a beloved pet to play the heaven card.

Putting aside for the moment the doctrinal issue of whether animals have souls, it's a comfort to be able to tell a small child that Bowser, Aunt Effie, or that nice old Mr. Johnson down the street has gone to heaven. If heaven is part of your faith, the comfort of heaven is certainly there for you.

But suppose that like many agnostics or secularists, you don't believe in a hereafter. Suppose you believe that heaven (and hell—let's not forget hell) is something we create for ourselves here on earth. Do you, in the stress of the moment, play the heaven card anyway? It's a question only you can answer.

### "Mommy, did all that stuff in the Bible really happen?"

Miracles are an everyday matter for little children. Their lives are filled with magic beans that grow into great beanstalks, frogs that turn into handsome princes, and comatose princesses who are brought back to life with a kiss. So they have no trouble granting full faith and credit to the miracles of the Bible.

But as they get older, they may want more than chapter and verse on the parting of the Red Sea and the life span of Methuselah. Parents who are of the belief that the Bible is the literal word of God have no choice but to affirm the authenticity of biblical miracles and let the credibility chips fall where they may.

Those parents who see Bible stories as subject to interpretation have a more challenging job: finding the wisdom in the stories of the Bible and getting it across to kids.

It may take some study and work, but we submit that it's study and work worth doing and will stand your kids in good stead as they work toward finding their faith.

### Apples roll

It's natural enough for parents to want their children to believe as *they* do and follow in their religious footsteps. Since the apple seldom falls far from the tree, that's usually what happens. But apples roll, and it's entirely possible that your child will find another way to answer The Big Question. If that should happen, your best option is acceptance.

**The fear factor**

Small children have great difficulty reconciling the loving God, whose eye is on the sparrow, with the wrathful God, who zapped Lot's wife into a pillar of salt. God, like parents, sometimes doles out severe punishment.

For example: Little Johnny is wakened by a terrible thunder-and-lightning storm (it doesn't help that he's been told that thunder is the sound of God moving His furniture). Terrified, he rushes into Mommy and Daddy's room screaming, "He's after me!"

"Who's after you, sweetie?" asks Mom.

"*God's* after me!" says Johnny.

"But, sweetie," says Mom, "God loves you very much!"

"Oh, yeah?" says Johnny. "Then how come He's after me?"

In this case, offering a more scientific explanation for nature's wrath might well be in order.

It's also tempting for hard-pressed parents to enlist God in their efforts to keep their kids reasonably in line. "God is watching you every minute, and He doesn't like it when you sass Mommy," says Mommy. It's not necessarily a great idea to use God for ordinary behavior modification. Not only is it like using a sledgehammer to swat a fly, it may even be a sacrilege.

But however you answer The Big Question and the multitude of questions that flow from it, it's as important to nourish a child's spirit and soul as it is his or her mind and body. It's a heavy responsibility. But whoever said raising kids was light work?

# SUMMING UP

There is a song in the musical *Annie* (lyrics by Martin Charnin, music by Charles Strouse) titled "You're Never Fully Dressed Without a Smile." We don't plan to write a song about it, but having raised two sons and closely observed the rearing of four grandchildren, we've come to believe that you're never fully adult without a child.

This is not to suggest that folks who have children are in any way superior to those who don't. Many of the greatest figures of history have been childless: Michelangelo, Spinoza, and Dr. Seuss, to name a few. It *is* to suggest, however, that there's nothing like parenthood to mature you beyond your years.

Though husbands and wives and life partners of all stripes and categories are responsible for each other, it is only parenthood that makes you fully and irrevocably responsible for another human being who is, for a time, utterly dependent—and as often as not, for another and another. (Johann Sebastian Bach, to look at the extreme end of things, had twenty children.)

A principal challenge of the parent-child relationship is that, in many ways, it is one-sided. That though your children are unquestionably yours, you are not necessarily theirs.

We have authority over our children, but once they've outgrown us, we've no real power except for the persuasive power of love and respect.

We are responsible for our children, but they are not responsible for us, unless they choose to be.

We are bound to our children for a lifetime, but once they are of age, and even before, they can slip those bonds whenever they choose.

So why do we set ourselves up for such a life-changing, all-consuming, one-sided relationship? The God of the Old Testament said, "Be fruitful and multiply," and that's an important but essentially unverifiable part of the "why." The verifiable part is that there is nothing else in life like the cry of a newborn smacked into squalling life, nothing like that squinched-up little face and those ten tiny fingers and ten tiny toes, nothing like your first realization that the small creature hanging on to your finger for dear life is a person like no other on earth and is destined to live a life like no other on earth.

So gather ye rosebuds while ye may, but hold yourself ready should that life-changing, all-consuming, thrilling experience of parenthood come your way.

# A COMPLETE GUIDE TO THE BERENSTAIN BEARS FIRST TIME BOOKS®

**The Berenstain Bears' New Baby**

Brother Bear outgrows his old trundle bed just in time for baby Sister Bear and achieves the exalted status of Big Brother as well as a fine new grown-up bed. A gentle conversation starter when Junior begins to notice that Mom's lap is getting smaller.

**The Berenstain Bears Go to School**

Wise Mama Bear helps Sister overcome her nervousness about starting school by taking her to visit Bear Country School in advance of the big day. An aid in overcoming resistance to going off to school for the first time.

## The Berenstain Bears Go to the Doctor

"Why do we have to go to the doctor for a checkup when we're not even sick?" complain the cubs. The cubs not only are declared "fit and healthy" by kindly Dr. Gert Grizzly, they show great courage in the face of booster shots. Help for hard-pressed parents when the kids drag their feet on the way to the doctor.

## The Berenstain Bears' Moving Day

Brother Bear is upset when Mama and Papa decide to move out of their mountain-cave home into a tree-house home deep in the valley. But with the help of his loving parents, Brother Bear manages to say goodbye to his old friends and looks forward to making new ones.

## The Berenstain Bears and the Sitter

The cubs are worried when a new sitter arrives for her first sit. But she turns out to be both a good cookie baker and a super bedtime-story teller. Help in getting children to accept a new sitter.

## The Berenstain Bears Visit the Dentist

Sister Bear's loose tooth provides Mama with an opportunity to get the cubs off to a good start with the dentist. Sister's non-traumatic visit to the dentist can help children accept their first dental examination.

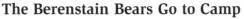

### The Berenstain Bears Go to Camp

The camp experience: from canoeing, to hiking, to bird-watching, to campfire stories atop spooky Skull Rock. Reassurance for kids who are about to have their first camp experience.

### The Berenstain Bears Get in a Fight

Brother and Sister get into a big fight. But when Mama Bear asks what they are fighting about, they can't, for the life of them, remember and peace is restored to the Bear family tree house. Conflict resolution for sibling squabblers.

### The Berenstain Bears in the Dark

When Sister Bear experiences fear of the dark at bedtime, Papa Bear gets out his old night-light, which comforted him when he was a cub. Aid and comfort for kids with night fears.

### The Berenstain Bears and the Messy Room

Cubs Brother and Sister find that the benefits of an orderly room far outweigh the work required to straighten up their messy, messy room. Help for the desperate parents of messy kids.

**The Berenstain Bears' Trouble with Money**

Brother and Sister Bear's approach to money management fluctuates wildly between spend-thrift behavior and miserliness. With Mama and Papa Bear's help, they find the sensible middle ground. An introduction to low finance.

**The Berenstain Bears and the Truth**

When Brother and Sister lie about how Mama's favorite lamp got broken, they learn that trust is not something that can readily be put back together once it's broken. Designed to help children resist the temptation to lie.

**The Berenstain Bears and Too Much TV**

When television viewing threatens to take over the cubs, mind and body, Mama institutes a no-television-for-a-week policy. Once Brother and Sister are over the shock, they discover a whole world of fun and knowledge beyond the boob tube.

**The Berenstain Bears and Mama's New Job**

Papa and the cubs feel slightly upstaged when Mama Bear decides to turn her quilt-making hobby into a business, but they decide that it's only fair for Mama to go into business if she wants to.

### The Berenstain Bears Meet Santa Bear

Mama Bear's wise approach to the mad run-up to Christmas helps Brother and Sister Bear understand that while toys, tinsel, and candy canes are fun, the holiday is really about peace and love. A gentle antidote to the overcommercialization of Christmas.

### The Berenstain Bears and Too Much Junk Food

The cubs reduce their intake of fattening, unhealthy food in response to Dr. Gert Grizzly's lecture on nutrition, health, and fitness. A cautionary tale for kids who are getting too big for their britches.

### The Berenstain Bears Forget Their Manners

When please and thank you are forgotten and rudeness threatens to take over the tree house, Mama posts a list of penalties for poor manners. At first the cubs mend their manners to avoid the penalties, but they soon learn to value good manners for their own sake.

### The Berenstain Bears Learn About Strangers

Mama and Papa instruct cubs Brother and Sister on the potential danger of being overfriendly with strangers. A conversation starter on a sensitive subject.

### The Berenstain Bears: No Girls Allowed

The gender wars visit Bear Country when Brother Bear and his friends shut Sister Bear out of their clubhouse. A rapprochement of sorts is achieved when Papa builds Sister and her friends a marvelous tree house.

### The Berenstain Bears and Too Much Birthday

Sister Bear learns that there's more to birthdays than cake and ice cream, presents and party games—there's the self-esteem that comes with growth and achievement and looking forward to the challenges of the years ahead.

### The Berenstain Bears Get Stage Fright

When Sister gets the main part in the school play, she's sure she'll be overcome by stage fright. But with the help and support of Mama and Papa, and lots of rehearsing, she does so well she can't wait to try out for the next play. Reassurance for future superstars.

### The Berenstain Bears and the Week at Grandma's

When cubs Brother and Sister hear that they are going to spend a whole week at Gramps and Gran's, they protest. "A whole week with Gramps and Gran— they're so *old*!" As it turns out, Brother and Sister have a grand time with "oldsters" Gramps and Gran.

### The Berenstain Bears Go Out for the Team

When Brother and Sister Bear try out for Little League, Mama and Papa are as anxious about it as the cubs. Brother is concerned that Sister may make the team while he may not. But with Mama and Papa's support, both cubs are welcomed to the Little League. An anxiety-reduction treatise for Little League kids and parents.

### The Berenstain Bears and the Trouble with Friends

When Sister complains that Lizzy is too bossy, Mama gently probes, asking if maybe Sister wasn't a bit bossy herself. There is a knock on the door. It's Lizzy. Sister left one of her best dolls behind and Lizzy thought she might miss it. Sister is touched and their friendship is restored. Friendship 101 for cubs and kids.

### The Berenstain Bears and the Bad Habit

Sister Bear has become a confirmed nail nibbler, and though she is eager to break the habit, she just can't seem to remember not to bite. Mama finds a way to help Sister remember and Sister gets her long, lovely nails back. An exploration of the nature of habits both good and bad.

### The Berenstain Bears' Trouble at School

Brother is missing school because he is home with a cold. But Teacher Bob is sending work home so Brother won't fall too far behind. Brother, however, ignores the work and lets his schoolwork slide with disastrous results. A parable that will resonate with every child and parent.

## The Berenstain Bears and the Bad Dream

Brother and Sister see a horror movie and indulge in scary play. The result: Sister has a nightmare and jumps into bed with Mama and Papa, who explain that daily events are often the stuff of dreams. An approach to helping kids understand where dreams come from.

## The Berenstain Bears and the Double Dare

When the Too-Tall gang steals Sister Bear's jump rope, Brother goes to get it back and is tempted by the blandishments of gang membership. But he sees the error of his ways and learns a valuable lesson. A gentle caveat about the power of peer pressure.

## The Berenstain Bears Get the Gimmies

Mama and Papa Bear give in when Brother and Sister throw a candy tantrum at the supermarket checkout. A case of the "galloping gimmies" ensues until the wisdom of Gramps and Gran is brought to bear and the crisis is ended. An approach to impulse control and to ameliorating the candy crisis at the checkout.

## The Berenstain Bears and the In-Crowd

Sister Bear is desolate when high-fashion Queenie puts down Sister's low-fashion pink-hair-bow look. Mama suggests a whole new look, but Sister stands up to Queenie and wins the day through spunk and smarts. A caution against going along to get along.

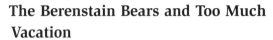

### The Berenstain Bears and Too Much Vacation

The Bear family finds out that the worst vacation they ever had is the one they look back on with the most joy and laughter.

### The Berenstain Bears: Trick or Treat

Brother and Sister and their friends go trick-or-treating and find out that scary-looking old Miz McGrizz not only is a sweet and lovely person but also gives out the best treats. An object lesson that appearances can not only be deceiving, they can be wrong.

### The Berenstain Bears and the Slumber Party

The twin issues of privilege and responsibility come to the fore when Sister's first sleep-over ends with the police being called. Mama and Papa learn that constant vigilance is key when granting privileges to the cubs.

### The Berenstain Bears and the Prize Pumpkin

Papa Bear is sad when "The Giant," a huge pumpkin he has raised, fails to win first prize at the Thanksgiving festival. Notwithstanding his loss, Papa recognizes that he has a lot to be thankful for: his family, their home sweet tree, and all the delicious pumpkin pies Mama will make out of "The Giant."

### The Berenstain Bears' Trouble with Pets

Mama Bear exacts a promise that cubs Brother and Sister will take care of the new pup if she agrees to pet ownership. It's touch and go for a while, but they manage to do so and learn something about responsibility in the process.

### The Berenstain Bears Don't Pollute (Anymore)

When woodsbear Papa scoffs at the cubs' environmental concerns, Professor Actual Factual intervenes. He takes Papa on a tour of environmental do's and don'ts. Papa learns the error of his ways and thereafter plants a tree for every one he chops down. Ecology 101 for kids.

### The Berenstain Bears and the Trouble with Grownups

When Mama and Papa come down too hard on the cubs, they dress up like Mama and Papa and put on a skit portraying them as being mean and bossy. Turnabout being fair play, Papa and Mama dress up like Brother and Sister and portray them in a less-than-favorable light. The result: improved mutual perspective.

### The Berenstain Bears and Too Much Pressure

When Mama Bear breaks down and cries out of frustration with the cubs' overloaded schedule, Papa intervenes and draws up a more manageable one. A little perspective for overscheduled families.

### The Berenstain Bears and the Bully

When Brother goes to the playground to "take care of" the bully that beat up Sister, he finds to his dismay that it's a girl. He decides that Sister needs a course in self-defense. A conversation starter on a difficult subject.

### The Berenstain Bears' New Neighbors

Papa Bear objects to the just-moved-in family of pandas because they look different. A visit with the panda family, who couldn't be nicer, gets crotchety Papa over his unfortunate lapse. An icebreaker on a touchy subject.

### The Berenstain Bears and the Green-Eyed Monster

Sister is green with envy when Brother gets a snazzy new bike for his birthday—so much so that she tries to ride it, with near-disastrous results. Papa then fixes up Brother's outgrown two-wheeler with training wheels for a mollified Sister.

### The Berenstain Bears and Too Much Teasing

At first Brother Bear is relieved when the Too-Tall gang shifts its cruel teasing from him to Milton Chubb, a non-athletic, overweight new cub. Feeling guilty about his sense of relief, he shows Milton how to use his special talents to defeat the Too-Tall gang. Addresses the issue of destructive teasing.

## The Berenstain Bears Count Their Blessings

Mama and Papa Bear become frustrated when Brother and Sister grow envious of their friends' possessions and suggest that the cubs should count their blessings instead. A really scary thunder-and-lightning storm breaks out, reminding the cubs of such blessings as their warm, cozy tree house, their loving parents, and hot cocoa by the firelight.

## The Berenstain Bears and the Homework Hassle

Papa Bear goes on the warpath when Brother falls behind in his homework. Brother sulks off and complains to Gramps and Gran. Their counsel helps Brother catch up. A countermeasure against kids' tendency to let homework slide.

## The Berenstain Bears and the Blame Game

Mama Bear institutes a policy of shared blame and instant cleanup when cubs Brother and Sister play the "blame game."

## The Berenstain Bears Get Their Kicks

Papa is so partial to baseball that he resents Brother and Sister Bear's excitement about soccer. After mocking the "kicking game," he discovers its merits and becomes a soccer dad.

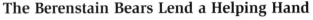

### The Berenstain Bears Lend a Helping Hand

When Papa volunteers the cubs to help old Miz McGrizz clean her attic, they are resentful but soon become fascinated with the story of old Miz McGrizz's life as told by the things in her attic, and they are well rewarded.

### The Berenstain Bears' Mad, Mad, Mad Toy Craze

A cautionary tale about getting caught up in every mad fad that comes along only to get left holding the bag—or the Chia Pet—and feeling foolish.

### The Berenstain Bears Think of Those in Need

When the cubs propose selling their extra stuff at a yard sale, Mama appeals to their better nature, and they feel very good about bestowing their largesse on various worthy institutions. A gentle prod to persuade cubs and kids to think of others.

### The Berenstain Bears and the Big Question

When Sister asks, "Mama, what's God?" Mama answers, "God is the creator of all things." But Sister has many more questions. As they head home from church, Sister has one last question: "Mama, did God make questions?" "Yes, my dear," says Mama. "Mostly questions."

**The Birds, the Bees, and the Berenstain Bears**

As Mama and Sister walk to Dr. Gert Grizzly's office, pregnant Mama comments on the facts of life. The birds and the bees 101.

**The Berenstain Bears and Baby Makes Five**

Sister Bear is jealous of the new baby. All the more so when Papa shows videos of the newborn. But wait! It's not the new baby in the videos, it's Sister when she was a baby and got all the attention. Sister sees the light and accepts the new baby.

**The Berenstain Bears' Dollars and Sense**

Cubs Brother and Sister are much better at spending their allowances than making them last. Mama establishes an in-house checkbook system that requires the cubs to keep track of their spending. Comes with tear-out checks so kids can use them just like the cubs do in Bear Country.

**The Berenstain Bears and the Excuse Note**

When Sister Bear uses the excuse of a twisted ankle to get out of sweaty old gym class, Mama points out that it's just as important to exercise your muscles as your mind. Sister accepts the logic and becomes a star performer in gym.

### The Berenstain Bears and the Big Blooper

The words cubs pick up today! Sister Bear brings home a lulu and says it at the dinner table in all innocence. When the shock wave has passed, Mama has a talk with Sister about the whys and wherefores of appropriate language.

### The Berenstain Bears' Report Card Trouble

Brother Bear is grounded after he ignores his studies in favor of his sports activity. He struggles to bring up his marks, but he has fallen so far behind that the whole family has to pitch in and help.

### The Berenstain Bears and the Real Easter Eggs

Cubs Brother and Sister get so carried away with Easter candy that they forget what the holiday is really about. But when they discover a nest of newly hatching robin eggs, they are reminded of the true meaning of Easter: the miracle of new life.

### The Berenstain Bears' Funny Valentine

With Mama's help, Sister learns that though some boys have a strange way of showing affection, their affections are nonetheless real. Comes with a special Bear Country Valentine's Day card.

**The Berenstain Bears and the Mama's Day Surprise**

Mama Bear likes her Mother's Day breakfast in bed, but what she really likes is the clean kitchen the cubs leave.

**The Berenstain Bears and the Papa's Day Surprise**

The cubs and Mama see through Papa Bear's put-down of Father's Day. They pretend to go along, but prepare a Father's Day celebration that warms his heart.

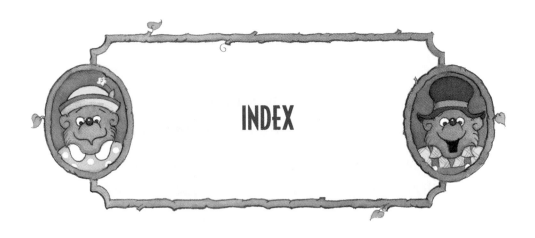

# INDEX

# ABOUT THE BERENSTAINS

Stan and Jan Berenstain have been drawing together ever since they met on the first day of art school in 1941. After Stan's three-year-plus army service during World War II, while Jan served on the home front as an aircraft riveter, they became cartoonists and cover artists for such magazines as *Collier's* and the *Saturday Evening Post,* as well as the parents of sons, Leo and Michael. They were writers as well as artists with *Berenstains' Baby Book,* the first of many books about everyday family life. Their eponymous Bears made their frolicsome debut in the spring of 1962 in *The Big Honey Hunt,* the Berenstains' first children's book. Illustrator/writer son Michael joined Team Berenstain in 1991. The Berenstains live and work in Bucks County, Pennsylvania, where they continue to create books about the Bear family, who lives in the big tree house down a sunny dirt road deep in Bear Country.